FITNESS
RUNNING

Third Edition

Richard L. Brown, PhD

Human Kinetics

FITNESS
RUNNING

Library of Congress Cataloging-in-Publication Data

Brown, Richard L., 1937-
  Fitness running / Richard L. Brown. -- Third Edition.
      pages cm
  Includes bibliographical references and index.
  ISBN 978-1-4504-6881-7 (print)
  1. Running. 2. Physical fitness. I. Title.
  GV1061.B77 2014
  613.7'172--dc23

                              2014023544

ISBN: 978-1-4504-6881-7 (print)

This publication is written and published to provide accurate and authoritative information relevant to the subject matter presented. It is published and sold with the understanding that the author and publisher are not engaged in rendering legal, medical, or other professional services by reason of their authorship or publication of this work. If medical or other expert assistance is required, the services of a competent professional person should be sought.

The web addresses cited in this text were current as of August 2014, unless otherwise noted.

Acquisitions Editor: Tom Heine; **Developmental Editor:** Carla Zych; **Managing Editor:** Elizabeth Evans; **Copyeditor:** Annette Pierce; **Indexer:** Dan Connolly; **Permissions Manager:** Martha Gullo; **Graphic Designers:** Nancy Rasmus and Tara Welsch; **Cover Designer:** Keith Blomberg; **Photograph (cover):** © Neustockimages/iStockphoto; **Photographs (interior):** © Human Kinetics; **Visual Production Assistant:** Joyce Brumfield; **Photo Production Manager:** Jason Allen; **Art Manager:** Kelly Hendren; **Associate Art Manager:** Alan L. Wilborn; **Illustrations:** © Human Kinetics, unless otherwise noted; **Printer:** Versa Press

We thank the Adidas Amazon Trail, the South Eugene High School, and the University of Oregon in Eugene, Oregon, for assistance in providing the locations for the photo shoot for this book.

Human Kinetics books are available at special discounts for bulk purchase. Special editions or book excerpts can also be created to specification. For details, contact the Special Sales Manager at Human Kinetics.

Printed in the United States of America   10 9 8 7 6 5 4 3 2 1

The paper in this book is certified under a sustainable forestry program.

Human Kinetics
Website: www.HumanKinetics.com

United States: Human Kinetics
P.O. Box 5076
Champaign, IL 61825-5076
800-747-4457
e-mail: humank@hkusa.com

Canada: Human Kinetics
475 Devonshire Road Unit 100
Windsor, ON N8Y 2L5
800-465-7301 (in Canada only)
e-mail: info@hkcanada.com

Europe: Human Kinetics
107 Bradford Road
Stanningley
Leeds LS28 6AT, United Kingdom
+44 (0) 113 255 5665
e-mail: hk@hkeurope.com

Australia: Human Kinetics
57A Price Avenue
Lower Mitcham, South Australia 5062
08 8372 0999
e-mail: info@hkaustralia.com

New Zealand: Human Kinetics
P.O. Box 80
Torrens Park, South Australia 5062
0800 222 062
e-mail: info@hknewzealand.com

E6145

To my wife Barbara, my daughter Jenny, and my son Steve,
who have shared their thoughts and supported me

Contents

PART III   Training Schedules

Preface

This third edition of *Fitness Running* is for people, at all levels of ability, who love to run or think they might like to start running.

Running is a natural, enjoyable, and productive activity that almost everyone can take part in. Our bodies are built to travel over the ground on two legs. Running connects us to the natural world and at the same time gives us a sense of freedom. Running allows us to "get away from it all" and to breathe deeply. It's a great way to explore a new city or town or to take a fresh look at our usual surroundings. When we run we notice things around us that we'd otherwise miss. Even when the weather is bad, by the end of a run we feel good. Running is the most natural way in the world to get fit or stay fit.

Fitness Running is organized into three parts. Part I, Running Readiness, offers insights into clothing, shoes, running form, and warm-up and cool-down techniques as well as information on the process of adaptation and the unique issues female runners face at various stages of life.

Maximal oxygen uptake, the most important measurement of running fitness, is explained in detail. An overview of low-tech and high-tech running gear is provided, along with advice on gearing up without spending a fortune. Running form is covered in depth. The pros and cons of wearing minimalist shoes and barefoot running are examined. Hans Selye's seminal general adaptation theory and its applications for everyone who runs or trains are presented in straightforward, practical terms.

Part II, Program Planning, guides you through the step-by-step process of using your own goals and characteristics to plan an effective running program. Here you learn about 10 types of running workouts, including new interval training, developed by Peter Thompson; what to do before and after a running workout; and why and how to cross-train and keep a running diary.

Details on stretching, nutrition, monitoring recovery indicators, and the science behind cross-training in water are provided.

Part III, Training Schedules, offers specific workouts that will help you reach the goals you want to achieve. Week by week, day by day, customizable programs for beginning training, fitness training, short-race training, half marathon training, and marathon training are laid out. The last chapter in this section covers postrace recovery and injury training, important parts of any running program, and arms you with suggestions for reenergizing and healing your body.

Intensity ranges are color coded so you can see at a glance how challenging each workout is likely to be. The schedules are flexible, and the intensity ranges are calculated and prioritized to fit your weekly and daily training needs. Offered in the margins beside the schedules are training hints or examples of effective, and a few not-so-effective, training and racing protocols.

My goal in creating this book is to help you make running an enjoyable and challenging part of your life, whether that means running on your own, enjoying fun runs, aiming for personal bests, or working to break into the ranks of the elite level. The principles outlined here can work for everyone. My hope is that you'll use the solid information retained from the previous editions and the considerable amount of new material in this edition to better enjoy your running experience and to improve your fitness and running ability.

Acknowledgments

I extend my thanks to Joe Henderson, my coauthor for the first two editions; to Peter Thompson for his professionalism and shoes; to photographer Eric Evans and models Christina Rogers, Jennifer Deluca, Diego Mercado, and Dan Kremske for their hard work; and to Jim Hill for providing the clothes for the models.

PART I

Running Readiness

Your body already knows how to run. Humans are a running species, and children become runners soon after their first steps. It's part of evolution and your ancestry. Although not all of us run on into adulthood, we are all familiar with the basic technique of putting one foot in front of the other at a faster-than-strolling pace.

So the question you want this book to answer isn't How do I run? It is How can I run better and make it a safe, consistent part of my life? The answer depends on who you are and what your goals are.

Maybe you ran track in high school, but that was years, and perhaps several pounds, ago. The longer it has been and the less active you've been, the longer and more carefully you must work to get back into running shape. But you can get there! This book will show you the path to safe, effective fitness running.

Perhaps you already run, but your daily 2-mile run through the neighborhood isn't as satisfying as it once was. Maybe you often feel physically or mentally flat. Maybe you are starting to notice nagging injuries. This book will show you ways to train without strain and ways to inject enthusiasm into your running.

Maybe you're running trouble free, but you'd like to get more from it. You see an announcement for a local 5K race and would like to enter. You'll see how enjoyable running can be when you train for a scheduled race and it becomes both a challenge and a social event.

You may already be racing and want to go farther or faster. Your goal is to improve your personal best in the 5K, to step up to the 10K next time, or to increase your distance all the way to the half marathon or marathon. This book will show you how to race safer and faster.

Part I of the book lays the groundwork for your running enjoyment and improvement. This section will help you

- assess your running health (chapter 1);
- select proper shoes, clothing, and other equipment to make your running safer and more comfortable (chapter 2);

- refine your running form so that you can move more efficiently (chapter 3);
- understand the essential concepts of Selye's general adaptation syndrome and learn to avoid overtraining (chapter 4);
- incorporate everyday habits and choices that allow your body to recover from and adapt to training (chapter 5); and
- take into account the training and performance implications of some of the differences between male and female runners (chapter 6).

Running Health Assessment

Your first task before beginning a running program is to determine your starting point. How healthy and fit are you? This question applies to both experienced runners and beginners.

The terms health and fitness aren't synonymous. Health is the absence of disease or injury. Fitness is the ability to perform a specific physical task. Although you might be healthy in the sense of being illness free and uninjured, you might still be unprepared for the performance requirements of running. Likewise, you can have the aerobic fitness necessary to run but still be unhealthy if you have a chronic disease or injury.

You can determine how fit you are by completing a short running fitness profile or a short but effective run–walk test. Keep in mind that these assessments are only as helpful as your input is accurate. If you ignore key items in your profile, overestimate your capabilities, or try too hard in the run–walk test you might start at a level that is too high, which can lead to problems and discouragement. To minimize problems, such as injury, illness, or overtraining, and maximize improvement, start at a level that is right for you. Be honest with yourself and let the results tell you where to begin.

Health and Fitness Profile

Take a moment to think about your health history and your fitness habits. Then read each of the following 15 questions related to health and fitness factors and choose the statement that best describes you. Enter the point value for each statement in table 1.1 to calculate your score, and use table 1.2 to determine your starting level for training.

1. **Cardiovascular health:** Evaluating cardiovascular readiness is a critical safety check before you start a vigorous activity. *Warning*: If you have a history of heart disease or if you are older than 35, enter a running

program only after receiving clearance and instructions from your doctor. Which statement best describes your cardiovascular condition?

- ☐ I have no history of problems. (3 points)
- ☐ Past ailments were treated successfully. (2 points)
- ☐ Some problems exist but need no treatment. (1 point)
- ☐ I am under medical care for cardiovascular illness. (0 points)

2. **Injuries:** This is an indicator of whether your musculoskeletal system can withstand starting a running program. If you have an injury that is temporary, wait until it heals before starting the program. If the condition is chronic, you may need to cross-train. Which of these statements best describes you?

- ☐ I have no current injuries. (3 points)
- ☐ I have a temporary injury, but it does not limit activity. (2 points)
- ☐ I have a temporary injury that limits activity. (1 point)
- ☐ I have an ongoing injury that prohibits strenuous training. (0 points)

3. **Illnesses:** Temporary or chronic conditions can affect, delay, or disrupt your running program. Speak with your physician if you are concerned that an existing illness could or should limit your ability to run. Which of these statements best describes you?

- ☐ I am not ill. (3 points)
- ☐ I have a temporary illness, but it does not limit activity. (2 points)
- ☐ I have a temporary illness that limits activity. (1 point)
- ☐ I have an ongoing illness that prohibits strenuous training. (0 points)

4. **Age:** In general, the younger you are, the more likely you are to be in good physical shape. Age affects the body's ability to perform physical activity and should be taken into account. In which age group do you fit?

- ☐ 25 years or younger (3 points)
- ☐ 26 to 40 years (2 points)
- ☐ 41 to 50 years (1 point)
- ☐ 51 or older (0 points)

5. **Weight and BMI:** Being overweight is a major contributor to poor fitness. Being overweight requires your heart to pump blood to a significant amount of fat tissue in addition to muscle tissue and organs. It also adds stress to the skeletal system, causes systemic inflammation, and increases blood viscosity, a predictor of cardiovascular disease.

Being significantly underweight also causes multiple stresses on your body, especially to hormonal function. Body mass index (BMI) uses your weight and height to describe body composition. Use figure 1.1 to see where you fit, or use one of the following formulas to calculate your BMI:

$$703 \times [\text{body weight (lbs)} \div \text{height}^2 \text{ (in)}] \text{ or body weight (kg)} \div \text{height}^2 \text{ (m)}$$

The relative amounts of fat and muscle tissue should also be considered. A well-muscled person might be considered overweight based on his or her weight or BMI value, while someone who falls in the ideal weight category might have little muscle tissue and too much fat tissue. If you think you are well-muscled or poorly muscled, adjust the BMI results accordingly. Where does your current BMI fall?

☐ 18.5-25 (3 points)

☐ 17-18.4 or 25.1-27.5 (2 points)

☐ 15-16.9 or 27.6-31.5 (1 point)

☐ Below 15 or above 31.6 (0 points)

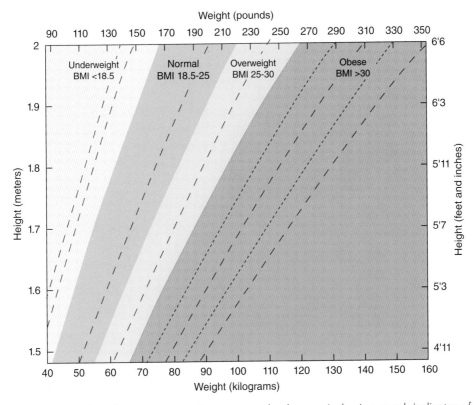

Figure 1.1 Although it is not a precise measure, body mass index is a rough indicator of body composition. The dashed lines mark subdivisions within the main categories.

6. **Resting pulse rate:** A well-trained heart beats more slowly and efficiently than one that's less fit. To determine your resting pulse rate, take it as soon as you wake up but before getting out of bed. You can take your pulse at the radial artery, close to the inside of your wrist near your thumb, or at the carotid artery, on the side of your neck under the back of the jaw bone. Gently place your index and middle fingers on the artery and count the beats you feel for 60 seconds. Which of these statements describes your current pulse rate on waking up but before getting out of bed?

   ☐ Fewer than 60 beats per minute (3 points)

   ☐ 60 to 69 beats per minute (2 points)

   ☐ 70 to 79 beats per minute (1 point)

   ☐ 80 or more beats per minute (0 points)

7. **Sleep:** Sleep is a key ingredient in recovery and improvement. Which of these statements best describes your sleeping habits?

   ☐ I sleep extremely well and get enough sleep. (3 points)

   ☐ I sleep OK and sometimes don't get enough sleep. (2 points)

   ☐ I sleep poorly. Often when I wake up at night it is difficult to get back to sleep. (1 point)

   ☐ I have significant sleep problems. (0 points)

8. **Nutrition:** A nutritious, balanced diet is another key ingredient in recovery and improvement. In many ways, you are what you eat. Your body knows the difference between a fast-food french fry and an organic apple. Which of these statements best describes your nutritional habits?

   ☐ I eat regular balanced meals, including breakfast. (3 points)

   ☐ More often than not, I eat a reasonably appropriate amount of nutritious foods. (2 points)

   ☐ I often eat unhealthy foods. I frequently eat too much or too little.

   ☐ My diet includes a lot of fat, sugar, and empty calories. I regularly eat too much or too little. (0 points)

9. **Smoking habits:** Smoking is an enemy of health and fitness. Which of these statements best describes your smoking history?

   ☐ I have never smoked. (3 points)

   ☐ I smoked but quit. (2 points)

   ☐ I smoke occasionally. (1 point)

   ☐ I smoke regularly. (0 points)

10. **Time available:** The time you have or can make available for running plays a role in setting running goals and your ability to achieve them. How would you describe the time you have to devote to fitness running?

☐ I have no limits on my time. (3 points)

☐ I have enough time. (2 points)

☐ I don't have as much time as I would like. (1 point)

☐ My time is very limited. (0 points)

11. **Support:** Your support system, including your family, friends, and coworkers, and your access to facilities play a role in setting running goals and achieving them. The best way to sum up support is to ask the questions, such as, is the person you live with happy to see you go out for a run or is the person upset when you go out for a run? How strong is your support system?

☐ I have an excellent support system. (3 points)

☐ I have a fairly good support system. (2 points)

☐ My support system could improve. (1 point)

☐ My support system is very poor. (0 points)

12. **Most recent run:** A good indicator of how well you will run in the near future is what you have run in the recent past. Which of these statements best describes your running in the past month?

☐ I have run nonstop for more than 4 miles (6.4 km). (3 points)

☐ I have run nonstop for 2 to 3 miles (3-5 km). (2 points)

☐ I have run nonstop for less than 2 miles (3 km). (1 point)

☐ I have not run recently. (0 points)

13. **Running background:** Running fitness isn't long lasting, but the fact that you once ran indicates that you might be able do it again. Which of these statements best describes your running history?

☐ I have run regularly within the past year. (3 points)

☐ I ran regularly one to two years ago. (2 points)

☐ I ran regularly more than two years ago. (1 point)

☐ I have never run regularly. (0 points)

14. **Related activities:** If you participate in other activities, they might contribute to running success. The closer the activity relates to running in terms of motion and aerobic benefit (such as bicycling, swimming, cross-country skiing, and fast walking), the better the carryover effect.

Which of these statements best describes your participation in other exercises that are similar to running in their aerobic benefit?

☐ I regularly practice similar aerobic activities. (3 points)

☐ I regularly practice less vigorous aerobic activities. (2 points)

☐ I regularly practice nonaerobic activities such as weight training and yoga. (1 point)

☐ I am not regularly involved in physical activity. (0 points)

15. **Level readiness:** What running level do you think you are ready to engage in? It is important to answer honestly. Don't be tempted to give the answer you wish were true.

☐ I am ready for challenging races. (3 points)

☐ I am ready to train for moderately challenging races. (2 points)

☐ I am ready for a fitness running program. (1 point)

☐ I am ready for the beginning training program. (0 points)

Table 1.1   Scoring Your Health and Fitness Profile

Enter your scores from your health and fitness profile.

Fitness category	Score
1. Cardiovascular health	
2. Injuries	
3. Illnesses	
4. Age	
5. Weight and BMI	
6. Resting pulse rate	
7. Sleep	
8. Nutrition	
9. Smoking habits	
10. Time available	
11. Support	
12. Most recent run	
13. Running background	
14. Related activities	
15. Level readiness	
Total score	

Table 1.2 Using Your Fitness Profile Score to Determine Your Starting Level

Total score	Recommended starting level
37-45	Start at any level
28-36	Start with half marathon, short-race running, or fitness running
19-27	Start with fitness running or beginning running
10-18	Start with beginning running
0-9	Discuss beginning a training program with a physician

Oxygen Efficiency and Running

Another way to determine where you might enter a running program is to determine your maximal oxygen uptake, or $\dot{V}O_2$max. This is often accomplished by a treadmill test, but it can also be done outside a laboratory setting using Cooper's 12-minute walk–run test, explained later in the chapter. Before we discuss the test, let's review how the body takes in and processes oxygen and the impact of oxygen efficiency on running and enjoying a healthy life.

Oxygen enters the lungs from the atmosphere by a pressure change created by the muscles in the rib cage and the diaphragm, which is a muscle under the ribs that causes the lungs to contract and expand. When the diaphragm goes up, the lungs contract and pressure increases, forcing air out of the lungs. When the diaphragm goes down, the lungs expand and pressure in the lungs decreases. Because the lung pressure is less than atmospheric pressure, air from the atmosphere rushes into the lungs (figure 1.2).

Try this quick check to see whether you are breathing properly: When you exhale your abdomen should go in, and when you inhale your abdomen should expand. If this is not the case, it might take a while to relearn belly breathing, which comes naturally to children. This will help you use oxygen more efficiently when you run.

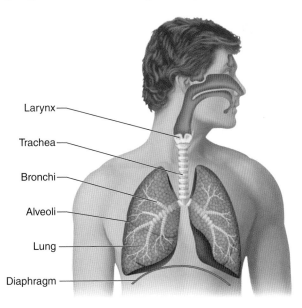

Larynx
Trachea
Bronchi
Alveoli
Lung
Diaphragm

Figure 1.2 When the diaphragm moves down, it helps draw oxygen into the lungs.

When the air enters the lungs, the oxygen is transferred through the alveoli to the red blood cells. The red blood cells contain hemoglobin, an iron-rich molecule that binds with the oxygen. The red blood cells make their way to the heart, where they are pumped out to the cells in the body through blood vessels.

The oxygen-rich red blood cells travel through increasingly smaller blood vessels until they get to the capillaries, very narrow blood vessels that pass by every cell. Because the red blood cells contain more oxygen than the cells in the body, the oxygen is released from the red cells into the cells of the body.

Once inside the cells, the oxygen finds its way to the cell's power plant: the mitochondria. The mitochondria produce energy to drive the work of the cell. Together the amount of oxygen you can provide the cells in your body and the ability of your mitochondria to use that oxygen determine an important measure of health and running fitness: $\dot{V}O_2$.

V stands for volume, O_2 is oxygen, and the dot above the V indicates over a period of time. Thus $\dot{V}O_2$ is a measure of the oxygen used in a specific amount of time. The units are milliliters per kilogram per minute (ml/kg/min).

Here is an example: Let's say a person who weighs 70 kilograms (154 lb) consumes 7,350 milliliters of oxygen while jogging easily for 10 minutes. What is the $\dot{V}O_2$?

$$7,350 \text{ ml} \div 70 \text{ kg} \div 10 \text{ min} = 10.5 \text{ ml/kg/min } (\dot{V}O_2).$$

The amount of oxygen used in this very easy jog, 7,350 milliliters, would almost fill four large water bottles (figure 1.3). At rest this person would probably use about 2,450 milliliters of oxygen.

$\dot{V}O_2$max is the maximum volume of oxygen a person can use per minute. As your $\dot{V}O_2$max increases, your fitness increases. Your $\dot{V}O_2$max is determined by both genetics and lifestyle. Many world-class runners have a $\dot{V}O_2$max that would remain above yours and mine, even if they were to stop running and we were to keep training hard—their genetic makeup is superior in this area.

As age increases, $\dot{V}O_2$max decreases, typically at about 10 percent per decade (figure 1.4). However, healthy sleep and nutrition habits and staying fit and active can slow the decline.

Figure 1.3 These four water bottles would hold about 8,000 milliliters of oxygen.

Let's compare two people who are the same age and both weigh 70 kilograms. One is in poor condition, with a $\dot{V}O_2$max of 30, and the other is in fantastic condition, with a $\dot{V}O_2$max of 80. They both complete a 10-minute run at maximal effort. Remember that oxygen used is directly related to energy converted. Therefore, more oxygen used means more energy is available for breathing and muscle movement. The energy converted is also directly related to the distance traveled. Table 1.3 shows the difference $\dot{V}O_2$max levels make in running performance. If $\dot{V}O_2$max represented a well of oxygen, it could be said that the extremely fit runner has a well 2.67 times deeper than the unfit person.

For our purposes, knowing your $\dot{V}O_2$max serves five important functions:

1. Reflects the health of the cardio-respiratory system
2. Accurately shows at what level to begin a running program
3. Measures progress
4. Suggests paces
5. Predicts performance

Figure 1.4 Physical activity slows the decline in $\dot{V}O_2$max that comes with age.

Jack Daniels, PhD, developed charts showing how $\dot{V}O_2$max, what he refers to as oxygen power, correlates with running performance. When I served as an exercise physiologist at Athletics West, the Nike track club in the late 1970s to mid-80s, we had a difficult time convincing the athletes that Daniels' charts were accurate. Then in one month Henry Rono ran a 3,000-meter world record (7:32), a 5,000-meter world record (13:08), and a 10,000-meter world record (27:22). On Daniels' chart each time correlated to a $\dot{V}O_2$max of 81.1.

Table 1.3   Impact of $\dot{V}O_2$max on Running Performance

	$\dot{V}O_2$max of 30	$\dot{V}O_2$max of 80
Oxygen available to be used per minute ($\dot{V}O_2$max × wgt × min)	21,000 ml	56,000 ml
Distance covered in 10 minutes	0.92 miles	2.48 miles

When you know your $\dot{V}O_2$max, you can figure out paces at different percentages of your maximum (table 1.4). Training at 60 percent of $\dot{V}O_2$max initiates the fight-or-flight response, which occurs when your body starts to react to a stressor. At this point you begin to achieve a training response. At 65 percent you begin to see a measurable cardiorespiratory response. At 75 percent you are well into the steady-state range, where you can continue for a long time and where your cardiorespiratory improvement is accomplished

Shelly Steely

Here's how I used $\dot{V}O_2$max with Shelly Steely, an athlete I coached from 1985 through 1996. Shelly made the World Championships in 1991 and 1993 and the Barcelona Olympics in 1992, where she was seventh in the 3,000 meters.

When we started working together, Shelly had a $\dot{V}O_2$max of 65 and could run the 3,000 meters in 9:09. She was able to run safely for only 250 minutes a week at 70 percent of $\dot{V}O_2$max. These measurements determined the **starting level** for our training program.

Even with an athlete as talented as Shelly, we were careful to train at a level that would keep her healthy. We recognized that patience is a valued asset. But by the time 1992 arrived she was able to train safely for 490 minutes a week at 84 percent of $\dot{V}O_2$max. Her $\dot{V}O_2$max was 72, and at the trials she ran the 3,000 meters in 8:41. We could **measure the progress** she was making through the years by tracking her $\dot{V}O_2$max.

Courtesy of Shelly Steely

Shelly Steely at the 1992 U.S. Olympic Trials.

We knew what **training paces** Shelly should use for various distances because we knew her $\dot{V}O_2$max. For example, in 1985 she could run 5 × 5 minutes at a pace of 80 seconds per 400 meters. In 1992 she could safely do 5 × 5 minutes at 75 seconds per 400 meters.

Knowing $\dot{V}O_2$max allowed us to select reasonable race goals. Just before the 1991 U.S. Championships, Shelly had run 4:08 for 1,500 meters, when her $\dot{V}O_2$max was 67.5. This allowed us to **predict that she was ready** to run 8:51 for 3,000 meters. Based on that prediction, we planned for her to run the first 60 percent of the race at an 8:51 pace and then see how she could finish. She was national champion in 8:47.

most efficiently. At 85 percent you are ready to pass the anaerobic threshold, the point where your body cannot produce enough energy aerobically and begins to produce energy anaerobically. At about 87.5 percent, you produce more hydrogen ions than your cells can deal with and lactate production is greater than lactate removal from the cells, which causes the pH of your cells to increase. At this point you begin to experience discomfort, and the "bear is about to jump on your back."

You can also estimate the percentage of $\dot{V}O_2$max you are reaching by gauging your perceived challenge, breathing rate, and ability to talk. Always remember to be honest and not brave in evaluating the level of challenge.

Finally, and perhaps most important, staying active yields $\dot{V}O_2$max benefits. Table 1.5 illustrates the age-related changes in $\dot{V}O_2$max of an inactive person compared to an active person. Both start at age 25 with a $\dot{V}O_2$max of 50.

The $\dot{V}O_2$max of the active 75-year-old person is almost 40 percent higher. Imagine how much better your cells can function with the additional oxygen available.

In review, $\dot{V}O_2$max is a good benchmark of fitness because it reflects the ability of the

1. lungs to remove oxygen from air,
2. blood to pick up the oxygen,
3. heart to pump the oxygen-laden blood,

Table 1.4   Relating Level of Effort to Percent $\dot{V}O_2$max

%$\dot{V}O_2$max	Status	Challenge	Breathing	Talking
60	Fight or flight	Moderate +	Noticeable -	Easy +
65	Cardiorespira-tory benefits	Strong -	Noticeable	Difficult -
75	Steady state	Strong	Deep, steady	Difficult
85	Anaerobic threshold	Strong +	Deep, rapid	Difficult +
87.5	Lactate buildup	Very strong	Deep, rapid +	Very difficult

Table 1.5   Effect of Activity on $\dot{V}O_2$max

Age	$\dot{V}O_2$max of inactive person	$\dot{V}O_2$max of active person
25	50	50
35	45	48
45	40.5	46.1
55	36.5	44.2
65	32.8	42.5
75	29.5	40.8

4. vessels to distribute the oxygen to all cells,

5. cells to extract the oxygen and deliver it to the mitochondria, and

6. the mitochondria to use the oxygen to produce energy and send carbon dioxide through the blood vessels to be expelled back into the atmosphere.

With this background information on oxygen and $\dot{V}O_2$max in mind, you are ready to test your fitness using the Cooper test.

Cooper's 12-Minute Run–Walk Test

Kenneth Cooper, MD, a leading authority in aerobic fitness, has long recommended a 12-minute run–walk test to estimate $\dot{V}O_2$max. The results of this test match up well with those obtained from sophisticated laboratory findings. Performing this test before you start one of the programs in this book will help ensure that you start at the level that is right for you. The same 12-minute test also is used later in the book to help you determine training pace.

First, note that if your results in the health and fitness profile indicate you should discuss with a physician starting a training program, you should not take this test. Second, this test will probably indicate a $\dot{V}O_2$max level a little lower than the results you would get through a test using a max treadmill test. However, it will be a safer test and a better experience because a max treadmill test pushes you to your highest aerobic capacity and with the equipment required is not always comfortable. I call the $\dot{V}O_2$max level obtained from this test your training $\dot{V}O_2$max. It is always better to start at a level that is too low than too high.

The goal of this test is to go as far as you can in 12 minutes. Take the test on a track or a flat stretch of accurately measured road. A standard running track is 400 meters, or 440 yards, and four laps equals either 1,600 meters, or 1 mile. You or an assistant will keep track of the distance you cover during the test. You can either time yourself or have an assistant time the test for you.

1. Before starting the test, warm up for 5 to 10 minutes by walking or jogging and performing dynamic movements such as jumping jacks. Do not do static stretches.

2. Start running at a pace you believe you can maintain for 12 minutes.

3. Walk if you feel you want or need to.

4. If possible, increase the pace slightly in the last 1 or 2 minutes.

5. Aim to feel tired, but exhilarated at the finish—not exhausted.

6. You should look forward with excitement, not with anxiety, to repeating this test later.

Look up the distance you covered in table 1.6 to see where you should begin your running program. If there is a difference between the recommendation associated with the score you achieved on the written fitness profile presented earlier in the chapter and the recommendation based on your score on the 12-minute test, use the recommendation from the 12-minute test.

If your score is low, don't be discouraged. Consider these two points: First, this test score is merely a starting point for your progress. The lower it is, the more room you have for improvement in later tests. Second, this result gives you a realistic basis for selecting training programs in this book. The programs must be based on your current ability. Table 1.7 presents a more complete picture of how the distances and paces relate to $\dot{V}O_2$max.

Knowing at what level to begin your training is a key to your running success. As you continue running, your $\dot{V}O_2$max will improve, and you can adjust your training accordingly by retaking the short quiz or performing another Cooper test. In part II we'll talk about using recent racing results to determine your new $\dot{V}O_2$max.

Table 1.6 Using Your 12-Minute Test Results to Determine Your Starting Level

Distance covered	Start category	$\dot{V}O_2$max
Less than 1 mile (1.6 km)	Consult physician	23.9 ml/kg/min or less
1-1.24 miles (1.6-2 km)	Beginning running	24-30.9 ml/kg/min
1.25-1.49 miles (2-2.4 km)	Beginning or fitness running	31-37.9 ml/kg/min
1.50-1.74 miles (2.4-2.8 km)	Fitness running to half marathon	38-45.9 ml/kg/min
1.75 miles or more (2.8 km)	Any level	46 ml/kg/min or more

Table 1.7 Determining $\dot{V}O_2$max Based on 12-Minute Test Results

Laps	Miles (pace min/mile)	Kilometers (pace min/km)	$\dot{V}O_2$max (ml/kg/min)
3.75	0.94 (12:46)	1.5 (8:00)	22
4	1 (12:00)	1.6 (7:30)	24
4.25	1.06 (11:19)	1.7 (7:04)	25
4.5	1.13 (10:37)	1.8 (6:44)	27
4.75	1.19 (10:05)	1.9 (6:19)	29
5	1.25 (9:36)	2 (6:00)	31
5.25	1.31 (9:07)	2.1 (5:43)	33
5.5	1.38 (8:42)	2.2 (5:27)	35
5.75	1.44 (8:20)	2.3 (5:13)	37

> continued

Table 1.7   Determining $\dot{V}O_2$max Based on 12-Minute Test Results > *continued*

Laps	Miles (pace min/mile)	Kilometers (pace min/km)	$\dot{V}O_2$max (ml/kg/min)
6	1.50 (8:00)	2.4 (5:00)	38
6.25	1.56 (7:42)	2.5 (4:48)	40
6.5	1.63 (7:22)	2.6 (4:37)	42
6.75	1.69 (7:06)	2.7 (4:27)	44
7	1.75 (6:51)	2.8 (4:17)	46
7.25	1.81 (6:38)	2.9 (4:08)	48
7.5	1.88 (6:23)	3 (4:00)	50
7.75	1.94 (6:11)	3.1 (3:52)	52
8	2 (6:00)	3.2 (3:52)	54
8.25	2.06 (5:50)	3.3 (3:45)	56
8.5	2.13 (5:38)	3.4 (3:31)	58
8.75	2.19 (5:29)	3.5 (3:25)	60
9	2.25 (5:20)	3.6 (3:20)	62
9.25	2.31 (5:12)	3.7 (3:15)	64
9.5	2.38 (5:03)	3.8 (3:10)	66
9.75	2.44 (4:55)	3.9 (3:05)	68
10	2.50 (4:48)	4 (3:00)	70

Running Gear

Part of the beauty of running is its simplicity. What could be more basic than lacing up a pair of running shoes, slipping into the right clothing for the conditions, and heading out your front door for a run?

Your essential equipment purchases for running are few and relatively inexpensive compared with most other sports. This chapter offers considerations and recommendations for choosing shoes, clothing, and accessories that enhance running safety, comfort, and enjoyment.

The list starts with shoes and, for a time, could end there. Even if you don't already run, your wardrobe probably includes most of the clothes you need to get started. Almost any light, nonrestrictive clothing will work early in your training. But you can't run well and safely in just any shoes.

Shoes

When running shoe models were all similar, runners used to be faced only with deciding which type of shoes were best and which of the most recent design changes and updates were worthwhile. But now, the choices include conventional shoes, minimalist shoes, and even no shoes. Following is background to help you make sense of the current options and decide what's best for you.

Evolution of Running

Let's take a moment to see what we can learn about running and running shoes from our ancestors. Before we had guns and vehicles, we humans hunted by chasing prey until they were exhausted. In this way, we evolved into excellent distance runners—initially without wearing shoes of any kind.

Along the way our feet evolved into a system of springs and levers that, when stretched, promote elastic recoil. The recoil is much like what happens to a stretched rubber band that releases energy when let go. Every time the foot hits the ground it stretches and during the recoil releases energy, which makes running more economical. The ligaments and tendons in the foot and ankle, the plantar fascia in the foot, and the Achilles tendon of the calf are parts of this powerful spring apparatus.

These parts of the foot, along with the skin, developed receptors to send messages to the brain, enabling the body to adapt to the forces placed on it during running. The messages encourage proper alignment, discourage injury, and enhance energy economy and biomechanical efficiency. The skin remained somewhat soft and receptors evolved to receive clues from the surface upon which the foot lands. Sweat glands also evolved in the foot to help dissipate the heat produced during running.

Humans use three types of movement to move from one place to another: walking or slow jogging, running, and sprinting. Typically, when we walk, we use a heel-to-toe movement; when we run, we use a midfoot-to-heel-to-toe movement; and when we sprint we use a forefoot-to-heel-to-toe movement.

As anyone familiar with runners and running knows, if you put in enough miles, eventually you will experience injury. So if we have evolved as runners, why are so many of us subject to injury? Maybe we are not running as nature intended. Maybe our shoes have something to do with it.

It seems clear that in many locations and for many reasons we need shoes. Shoes protect the foot from the environment. While our earliest evolutionary relatives did run barefoot, they progressed to wearing light footwear such as sandals and moccasins. Although we can't know for sure, they apparently ran safely in them because these types of footwear endured over time.

It is certainly possible that the running shoes worn in recent decades provide too much protection and too much compensation for perceived deficiencies. Maybe many of these shoes, with their motion control and thick, shock-absorbing soles, hinder our natural movement and reduce the feedback to the brain. This may not only limit our potential, but may also promote injury.

Barefoot Running

While running barefoot may not be practical or safe for all people in all environments, it has sparked debate about not only what to wear to run but how to run. One observation scientists are still sorting out is whether there is a major difference between barefoot running and running with conventional running shoes. Experienced barefoot runners tend to strike the ground on the ball of the foot and then go back to the heel (figure 2.1a), whereas runners who wear conventional shoes tend to strike the ground with the heel first (figure 2.1b), sometimes even placing the heel ahead of the body (figure 2.1c), a maneuver known as overstriding. This observation that faster, more experienced runners strike the ground differently has led many runners to change their running form as well as their running shoes. In chapter 3 we discuss how foot strike relates to running form. Here we focus on the relationship between foot strike and shoe construction.

To appreciate the role of the foot strike in the design of running shoes, we need to understand the effect of the foot strike on the muscles. Concentric contractions of the muscle occur when you shorten a muscle, as when you do a curl with a weight and decrease the angle at the elbow. Eccentric muscle contractions occur when the muscle contracts while it is becoming longer, as when you hold a weight that is too heavy and you struggle to keep your elbow at a 90-degree angle. The weight causes the arm muscles to lengthen, even while the muscle is trying to contract, and the angle at the elbow to extend beyond 90 degrees. Exercise-induced muscle damage is greater with eccentric contractions than with concentric contractions.

As the foot hits the ground while running, the leg muscles decelerate the downward movement. At this point, not only is the body absorbing the shock of hitting the ground, but it is also experiencing eccentric muscle contractions. Rolling over the ground on your forefoot with a smooth stride like a wheel, rather than striking the ground with your heel in front of your body's center of gravity, distributes the force. When the forefoot hits the ground, it transmits less force up through the body than when the heel strikes the ground. The force of hitting the ground, which is 2 to 3 times a person's body weight, is less when landing on the forefoot. And landing on the heel can cause impact twice, the first when the heel hits the ground and the second when the rest

Figure 2.1 (*a*) Forefoot strike (*b*) heel strike, and (*c*) extreme heel strike.

of the foot hits the ground. Although the eccentric contractions at the ankle during the forefoot strike is higher than during heel strike, the eccentric contractions around the knee are more than three times less.

There is no question that most runners are heel strikers. This may be because more people run slowly than run fast. Although heel striking is more efficient than forefoot striking at a 7:36-per-mile pace (4:43/km), by the time the pace nears 6:25 per mile (3:59/km), forefoot striking is more efficient. The recent debate on foot strike suggests that the heel strikers have more hip and knee injuries, while forefoot strikers have more Achilles tendon and plantar fascia injuries.

Because the foot hits the ground about 1,000 times in a mile (1.6 km) run, it would be nice to have more definitive answers about which foot plant is best. But it seems that in many ways we are each individuals when it comes to foot strike. While many experts advise you to let your foot do its own thing, many point out that *where* your foot hits the ground is more important than *how* it hits. They recommend that you avoid overstriding, which interrupts the wheel-like motion of running. The body perceives overstriding as putting on the brakes, which interferes with the rotational movement of the lower extremities. When you overstride, you must overcome inertia with each foot plant.

Runners who land on the forefoot do not need the same type of shoe as heel strikers. Measurements of shoes manufactured in 2013 show the average difference between the amount of material used in the heel and in the forefoot of the shoe's sole was 10.4 millimeters (ml). The biggest difference was 14.4 ml. More minimal shoes, which forefoot-strikers can wear, averaged a difference of only 2.4 ml. This number is closer to the difference in conventional shoes of the late 1960s and early 1970s.

We can't ignore the fact that many more people are now running than they were in the 70s. But neither can we ignore the fact that since the 70s shoes have changed in ways that encourage heel striking and restrict natural motion of the foot. Studies are needed to determine the best way to protect the foot without restricting it. No conclusive evidence supports the advantages and disadvantages of running barefoot or in minimalist shoes instead of in conventional shoes.

Some advocates suggest that running barefoot or running in minimalist shoes reduces the incidence of some types of overtraining injuries, notably those affecting the knees and hips. Others agree that this might be true but suggest that it also causes an increase in different injuries. Some sports medicine doctors have noticed an increase in Achilles tendinitis and metatarsal stress fractures associated with running barefoot or in minimalist shoes, especially if the transition to that form of running occurs too quickly or if the runner is a heel striker.

People who run in Vibram FiveFinger or similar shoes and transition slowly still have increased bone marrow edema, suggesting inflammation of the lining of the joints. This swelling can make it painful to run. It appears that the transition to a minimalist shoe or barefoot running is initially stressful to the bones of the foot. If runners want to try this type of running, and millions of minimalist shoes have been sold, they should make a gradual transition.

Running with minimalist shoe, regardless of foot strike, is marginally more energy efficient than running in conventional shoes. The difference is probably caused by more elastic energy storage and release in the lower extremities. Reduced shoe weight and better sensory feedback could also play a role.

"More research is needed" seems to be a consistent takeaway. A second takeaway is that each of us is different and we have different footwear needs. A final conclusion is that the way people run, forefoot strike vs. heel strike, is often more important than what they wear. Runners should learn efficient form and then select shoes that help them safely accomplish their goals. Efficient form is discussed in the next chapter, so for now let's continue to talk about shoes.

Parts of the Shoe

In addition to knowing how your foot works while running, knowing about shoe construction can help you choose the right shoe. Let's look at some of the key parts of the shoe.

1. **The last:** The last determines the shape of the shoe. It includes the shape of the foot bed where you place the foot and the outer layer of material that covers the sides and top of the foot, called the upper. The three basic shapes are straight, semicurved, and curved (figure 2.2). Conventional wisdom says certain lasts are best for certain feet. Straight is suggested for people who

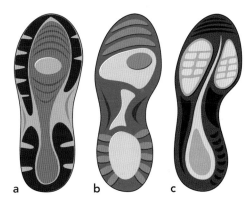

Figure 2.2 Types of lasts: (a) straight, (b) semicurved, and (c) curved.

overpronate or have flat feet (figure 2.3a). This shape helps control inward rotation. Semicurved is recommended for runners who are neutral pronators (figure 2.3b). A curved last serves runners who underpronate and have high arches (figure 2.3c).

Pronation is the position of the foot as it strikes the ground. Normal pronation helps absorb the shock of landing. If you overpronate, your foot rolls inward too much and you risk injuries, especially to the knees. If you underpronate, or supinate, your foot tends to roll outward too much and you risk injuries, especially to your feet.

Depending on the shape of the last, shoes are constructed with either a board last, slip last, or combination last. Straight-lasted shoes

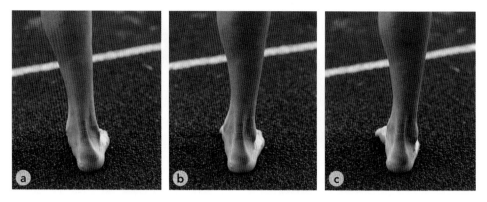

Figure 2.3   (a) Overpronation, (b) normal pronation, and (c) underpronation.

use a board last, which is a piece of fiberboard glued to the midsole. It is stiff and helps limit inward rotation. Curve-lasted shoes are built with a slip last, which is soft sock glued to the midsole. It is flexible and helps compensate for outward rotation. A combination-lasted shoe uses stiff fiberboard in the rear of the shoe and a sock in the front of a semicurve-lasted shoe.

2. **The sole:** The outersole of a shoe touches the surface you run on (figure 2.4a). Outersoles are usually made of a denser, harder material for the heel and a lighter material for the forefoot. Varying these substances allows shoe manufacturers to meet various requirements. For example, is the shoe to be worn for training, racing, trail runs, or road running? The midsole sits between the outersole and the foot bed. Single or multiple layers of vinyl acetate in various densities are usually used for the midsole.

3. **The upper:** The upper is the part of the shoe above the midsole that covers the foot (figure 2.4b). When you select a shoe, take into consideration what the upper is it made of and whether it dries in a reasonable time, is washable, and whether it breathes.

4. **Heel counter and toe box:** The heel counter is a stiff structure around the heel that adds cushioning, support, and rotational control (figure 2.4c). A correctly constructed and fitting toe box allows the toes to flex and spread as the foot leaves the ground (figure 2.4d). If the toe box is too narrow, it affects the natural movement of the foot and the messages sent to the brain.

5. **Flexibility:** Flexibility in a shoe allows the foot to move in a natural way. Look at the outersole to see whether it has flex grooves and then try to bend the forefoot area (figure 2.4e). Many years ago when I worked for Athletics West, the Nike running club, I tested a shoe called the Tailwind. It was made for pronators and for the most part worked well, but it was very stiff. I took a hacksaw and cut grooves

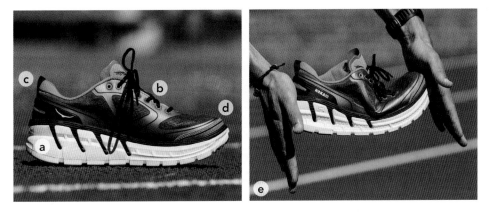

Figure 2.4 Parts of a running shoe: *(a)* the sole; *(b)* the upper; *(c)* the heel counter; *(d)* the toe box; *(e)* flexibility of shoe.

across the forefoot, which made it very flexible and much better to run in. Now you see grooves in many of the shoes sold today. I should have shown mine to somebody at Nike!

Selecting the Right Shoe

Before you buy a running shoe, preferably at a running specialty store, where most of the employees are runners and have been trained to match customers with the right shoe, be prepared to answer some questions:

1. Do you want conventional or minimalist shoes?
2. What kind of running will you use the shoes for and what type of surface will you run on?
3. How many miles will you run each week in these shoes?
4. How much do you weigh and how tall are you? Your body mass index can help identify the best shoes for you. Refer to figure 1.1 to find your approximate BMI or use this formula:
   - For English units use $703 \times$ [body weight (lbs) $\div$ height^2 (in)]
   - For metric units use body weight (kg) $\div$ height^2 (m)
5. What is your running injury history?
6. What type of arch do you have? To find out, get your foot wet and then stand on a dry surface. Compare your footprint to figure 2.5.

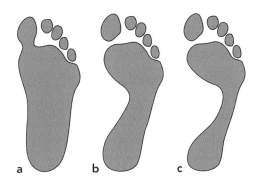

Figure 2.5 Arch types: *(a)* flat, *(b)* medium, and *(c)* high.

Some people say that the best way to determine whether a shoe is right for you is simply to step into it; the way it feels on your foot tells you whether it is right. I would add that if it still feels good after you run a few miles over a few days, it is the shoe for you—and you should buy a couple of pairs.

Remember, what is right for your friend may not be right for you. Any shoe you get should have an arch that matches your own, a heel that is snug but not tight, and a toe box wide enough to allow your toes to spread at push off. It should allow as much natural foot movement as possible while protecting you from the environment and allowing for sensory feedback.

Types of Shoes

The best way to get shoe information is to search the Internet for running-shoe reviews. Shoe companies produce new models frequently, so what you bought last year might not be available this year. Once you have an idea of what you're looking for, visit a specialty running store where you can speak with the staff and check out the actual products for yourself.

The differences between minimalist and conventional shoes are significant. Minimalist shoes are lighter, and the difference between the heel height and the forefoot height is small. They provide less cushioning and are much more flexible. You can usually twist these shoes on the long axis because they include little or no arch support.

Conventional shoes are heavier, and the difference between the heel height and the forefoot height is greater. This difference might encourage heel striking. Conventional shoes provide more cushioning and less flexibility. Because of the rigid arch support in many of these shoes, you can't twist them longitudinally. These shoes provide more motion control, which some runners appreciate because it can limit excessive pronation. But they also tend to decrease the sensory feedback that might otherwise alert runners to a pronation problem.

Manufacturers are plentiful and new shoe types are produced yearly by new and established shoe manufacturers. Tables 2.1 and 2.2 give you an idea of ranges and averages of various characteristics of conventional and minimalist running shoes.

Table 2.1 Conventional Running Shoes

	Low	High	Average
Price ($)	100	175	117
Heel height (mm)	21.9	38.7	34.0
Forefoot height (mm)	17.5	28.2	23.6
Height difference (mm)	2.1	14.4	10.4
Weight: men's (oz)	8	12.8	10.3
Weight: women's (oz)	6.4	10.4	8.5

Based on data from R. Loda, 2013, Best running shoes of 2013, spring edition. [Online]. Available: www.runningshoesguru.com/2013/03/best-running-shoes-of-2013-spring-edition [July 16, 2014].

Table 2.2 Minimalist Running Shoes

	Low	High	Average
Price ($)	85	195	125
Heel height (mm)	10.5	23.5	17
Forefoot height (mm)	10.5	19.7	14.6
Height difference (mm)	0	3.8	2.4
Weight: men's (oz)	6.2	8.7	7.9
Weight: women's (oz)	5	7.3	6.4

Based on data from R. Loda, 2013, Best running shoes of 2013, spring edition. [Online]. Available: www.runningshoesguru.com/2013/03/best-running-shoes-of-2013-spring-edition [July 16, 2014].

After the Purchase

Even when you buy the right shoe, you still need to deal with several aspects of shoe wear and care to enhance your running experience.

Break-in period: Even well-made running shoes require a break-in period. You should be able to put on a new pair and run without getting blisters, but any new shoes will cause your feet to hit the ground differently than they did in the old pair. You may develop soreness in your feet and legs while adapting to this change, so wear the new shoes only during easier runs until you've adapted. You can even start out by walking for a few days in the new shoes.

Rotation: Each brand and model, and even each pair of the same model, cause slightly different stresses on the feet and legs. By rotating shoes, much as you would tires on a car, you even out these stresses. Buying two or more pairs of shoes and switching off frequently is well worth the cost.

Care: Periodically, you should clean your running shoes and inspect them for signs of wear. Well-used running shoes get dirty and retain an odor. Because they're made mostly of synthetic materials, they can be washed. Hose them off frequently or throw them into the washing machine on a gentle cycle, but let them air dry—putting them in the dryer causes heat damage.

Running shoes commonly wear in two ways. Not only do the soles and heel grind down, but also the cushioning materials in the midsole fatigue and compress. You can repair the outer surfaces, but the shoe won't be much good if compression changes the shape and thickness of the sole. Opinions differ significantly regarding when to replace running shoes. Some say they should be replaced after as few as 250 miles (402 km). Others say you can go up to 1,000 miles (1,601 km). It depends on factors such as your body weight and composition, how your body moves, the surface you run on, and what type of shoes you have. You should inspect your shoes every month or every 100 miles (161 km) and note the changes in compression and use patterns on the soles.

Inserts: You can make a good shoe better by inserting protective devices. These include insoles to replace those that come with the shoe, upgraded arch supports, heel cushions, and custom-made shoe inserts called orthotics. The first three products are sold over the counter in sport and specialty stores, and the orthotic inserts are prescribed by a doctor. Use these devices only if you are troubled by injuries. Try to find devices made as light and as flexible as possible.

Other Equipment

Although they are most important, shoes are not the only equipment that will make your running safer and more enjoyable. Let's take a look at other items that can affect your running experience.

Clothing

Just as running shoes are designed to keep you comfortable by cushioning your feet against hard, jarring surfaces, running clothing is made to keep you comfortable in weather extremes. Modern fabrics make running tolerable in all but the harshest conditions. But two traditional fabrics perform well: cotton and wool. Wool wicks moisture well, dries quickly, and doesn't retain odors. It is warm on cold days and breathes nicely on warm days, which reduces swings of body temperature. And it needn't be heavy or bulky. Today it can be made into lightweight, smooth fabric. Table 2.3 compares wool with synthetic fabrics.

Whether you outfit yourself from a specialty store or with items you already own, include the following in your running wardrobe:

- Underwear that supports without binding
- Socks that don't slide down and bunch up in your shoes, which can cause discomfort and blisters
- Shorts that allow freedom of movement and don't chafe your inner thighs
- Shirts for different seasons—turtleneck, long sleeved, short sleeved, and sleeveless—in a variety of fabrics and weights

Table 2.3   Pros and Cons of Wool and Synthetic Fabrics

Quality	Wool	Synthetic Fabrics
Wicking	Excellent	Excellent
Drying time	Good	Excellent
Temperature regulation	Very good	Fair to good
Odor retention	Little	Significant
Elasticity	Very good	Very good
Price	Expensive	Moderate

- Gloves, mittens, or socks to keep your hands warm. Socks work well because all fingers and the thumb help warm each other. When I lived in Maine I usually ran 5 miles (8 km) every day. The temperature was often well below 0 degrees Fahrenheit (18 °C). I always wore cotton socks on my hands. About 4.5 miles into the run I took off the socks because my hands were too warm.

- Headwear for various weather conditions—a stocking cap for cold; a face mask (balaclava) for wind and cold; and a cap with a visor to shield you from rain, sun, and blinding headlights

- Tights that protect against the cold and don't get baggy and heavy in the rain

- Sweatpants, wind-resistant jackets, and weatherproof suits—jacket and pants—to keep you comfortable in the worst conditions

- A lightweight covering for the neck and chest. This item is rarely mentioned, but it is important in cool or cold weather. The bronchial tubes are a pathway to the lungs, and they contain cilia, which are tiny hairlike structures that protect the lungs by moving microscopic debris and dust particles up toward the mouth. They work well at body temperature, but are less effective when the temperature drops. On cold days it makes sense to assist the cilia by wearing clothing that protects the throat and upper chest. A turtleneck dickey serves that purpose with very little weight or constriction (figure 2.6). On a cold day one winter in Eugene, Oregon, I asked about 20 runners to dress the same way, with one exception: 10 wore a turtleneck dickey. When they got back we looked at their necks and upper chests. The 10 without the dickey were pale and cold to the touch. The upper chest of the other 10 was a nice pink color and that area felt warm. It is my belief that keeping that area warm helps prevent colds because it lets the cilia do their job.

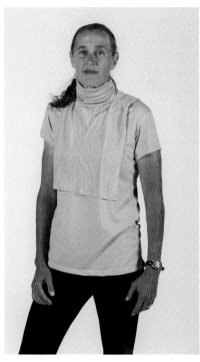

Figure 2.6 Turtleneck dickey.

Layers of light, breathable clothing are advantageous in cold and cool weather. If partway through the run you feel too warm, you can always take layers off. But if you go out without enough clothes and you feel too cold, you will stay cold.

Electronic and Digital Devices

A digital watch is an important tool. This inexpensive piece of equipment has a stopwatch feature that gives you instant, accurate information. GPS systems are becoming popular and are often incorporated into digital watches. They can track how far you run and at what pace. Some also estimate minute-by-minute heart rate and total heart rate.

For entertainment while running, many people use a smart phone or audio player to listen to music, news, and audiobooks. Listen to this type of device only when you know you will be safe from traffic. If you run on the street, be warned that wearing headphones or ear buds will tune in your music and tune out traffic noises.

The heart rate monitor also provides feedback about your runs. It registers the level of effort that you put into a workout. A lot of research has been published regarding heart rate training zones. The most accurate material focuses on using your heart rate reserve, which requires that you know your maximum and resting heart rates. These change frequently so interpretation is not always reliable.

Heart rate reserve is your maximum heart rate minus your resting heart rate. If two people had a max heart rate of 180 and one had a resting a heart rate of 50 and the other a resting heart rate of 80, their heart rate reserves would be 130 and 100, respectively. If both wanted to do a training session at 50 beats higher than their resting heart rate, the first people would work at 100 beats per minute or 55 percent of max heart rate and the second at 130 beats per minute or 72 percent of max heart rate. Basing workouts on heart rate reserve is more accurate than basing it on max heart rate. While it is true that over time max heart rate declines and resting heart rate mirrors health, max heart rate and resting heart rate change more frequently than one might think. Many aspects of life, such as rest, diet, recovery, and previous exercises, factor into the temporal value of these rates. I have used a machine that records several parameters of daily health, including max heart rate and heart rate reserve. What I learned from these factors varied on a daily basis even though we took readings at the same time of day.

I was an early fan (1978) of monitoring heart rate, but I have come to believe that if you are in tune with your body, you can monitor the intensity without electronic equipment. I once coached a masters athlete who wanted to qualify for the Boston Marathon. He was about 15 minutes over the qualifying time. When we talked on the phone he always started the conversation with his heart rate results. I felt that his fixation on the heart rate zones was a disadvantage to him because he went into the workout wondering if he could maintain a certain heart rate instead of reading his body and reacting to it. Some days it is a disadvantage to use heart rate because your body may not be ready for the level demanded. If he tried to reach a level over his head that day he would be a step closer to overtraining. I was frustrated that he was not improving as he should. One day he told me that the heart rate monitor stopped working. I said, "Don't get it fixed!" He lost his fixation on heart rate and started to improve. He qualified for Boston.

More sophisticated devices are on the horizon that will transmit information from the body to smart phones and computers. Smaller and smaller devices will be the goal for the companies producing them. But, as with the masters runner trying to qualify for Boston, many runners learn to stay in touch with their body in a more intimate way. Without devices you can train well, meet personal goals, and enjoy your running.

Sunglasses, Visors, and Hats

Let's end by talking about low-tech items. Sunglasses' tinted lenses reduce dangerous and annoying glare and help prevent eye damage in bright sunlight. Polarized lenses protect your eyes from both types of harmful ultraviolet: long wavelength and short wavelength. Visors and hats also help reduce glare and protect your skin from harmful sun rays.

Adding It All Up

How much you will spend on your running gear depends on how fully and stylishly you want to be outfitted and what your technology threshold is. You may already own clothing that you can run in, and you may have no interest in taking advantage of the latest electronic breakthroughs. On the other hand, you might be more motivated to run or find running more enjoyable if you're dressed in fashionable, ultracomfortable clothing and using the most recent technological devices on the market. Good-quality products are available in several price ranges; if you are willing to shop around, you should have no trouble finding what you need to get started at a price you can afford.

A word to the wise: Regardless of your sense of style, technological aptitude, and budget, let fit and comfort be your top priorities, especially when it comes to running shoes.

You have many options when it comes time to shop for equipment. Start with the running stores and sporting goods stores in your area. Not only are these establishments likely to offer a wide range of products at various price points, they also are likely to be staffed by people who have firsthand knowledge of the products and who are qualified to help you get a good fit. Unless the return policy allows for trial and error, steer clear of ordering items you are not already familiar with from an online retailer.

Here's a list of the running gear for a year-round runner. I have included price ranges in U.S. dollars from athletic specialty stores, but you can probably find some of these items for less at other stores.

Running Gear

Shoes: Training $90 to $190

Tempo and racing: $90 to $160

Running shorts: $24 to $55

Running shirts: $20 to $80

Supportive briefs: $30 to $60

Running bra: $20 to $75

Merino wool shirts: $50 to $85

Sweatsuit top: $40 to $150

Sweatsuit pants or tights: $40 to $120

Rain suit jacket: $40 to $190

Rain suit pants: $50 to $70

Running vest: $40 to $140

Wind-resistant jacket: $30 to $60

Cold-weather hat: $10 to $25

Gloves: $12 to $45

Sunglasses: $50 to $300

Visor or cap: $10 to $25

Digital watch, heart rate monitor, or smartphone: $50 to $300

Neck gaiter: $30 to $35

Turtleneck dickey: $10 to $15

Total: $716 ($736 including a bra) to $2,105 ($2,180 including a bra)

Don't skimp when purchasing shoes, wool tops, a good wool Navy watch cap, and a turtleneck dickey. There are fabrics that wick moisture from the skin and also serve as a base lay, but wool is still my fabric of choice. Just old school, I guess. These are key items, and quality makes a difference. To keep costs down, you can buy inexpensive socks, shorts, T-shirts, sweat pants, and caps and a basic watch. And you can use cotton socks for gloves. All these items work well. Just remember on cold days to dress in layers.

That being said, the low-end cost for the items I listed would be just a little over $700. You don't have to buy all the products, but it doesn't sound like a lot when you think of it as a "health insurance policy" investment. A "helping you feel good" investment. A "helping you look good" investment. After all, the only real miracle drug is physical activity, and running is an easy, portable physical activity you can do anywhere in all sorts of weather, alone or with friends.

Running Form

Running is natural—you've probably been doing it all your life! But most of you would hesitate to state unequivocally that your running form allows you to move in the fastest, most efficient manner possible, with the least chance of injury. Small mistakes in the way you run can penalize you, especially as your distance and speed increase. For this reason, it's worthwhile to review the basic concepts of good running form.

Although running form covers a wide range of personal differences, some general concepts apply to everyone from sprinters through marathoners.

1. Form must fit your individual characteristics. A small person, for instance, should not attempt the same stride length as someone a head taller.
2. Form changes with the pace. The faster you go, the closer you land to the forward part of the foot, the greater your hip extension, and the more you drive with your arms.
3. Form must be mechanically efficient. Mechanical efficiency enhances speed and reduces the risk of injury. Humans are upright animals and run best that way—with a straight back and eyes looking forward, not with a bent back and eyes looking down.
4. Form must be relaxed. Running with tension is like driving a car with the brakes on—it causes you to work harder but go slower.

This chapter looks closely at the mechanics of sound running form in every phase—the landing, the support, and the drive—and offers tips for improving form from the feet to the head.

Feet and Ankles

Chapter 2 discusses how foot strike affects shoe selection. Because the foot strike is more important than the shoes, here we cover proper form during foot strike.

A key point is that heel striking is less efficient than landing on the forefoot. The heel strike requires the body to absorb more force. The ankle and arch of the foot become less elastic and the muscles and ligaments supporting them are used less so they may become less efficient. During heel strike, the foot often hits the ground in front of the center of gravity, causing the leg to act as a brake, which means you must regain momentum after each foot strike. Finally, the sensory feedback system is less efficient during heel striking because the nerve endings in the heel are sending indirect or muffled messages to the brain. The nerve endings in the forefoot have evolved to send those messages more efficiently. In my opinion, based on my own running as well as my experience coaching many athletes and observing numerous others, landing on the forefoot is best for safe and efficient running, especially when running at faster speeds.

Heel Strike

If you are running at a pace of 8 minutes per mile (4:48 min/km) or slower, you will probably land on your heels. If you don't want to try the midfoot or forefoot strike or don't think you are ready for it, make sure your heels contact the ground under your center of gravity and not in front of it.

Landing

This phase is the period from touchdown to when the whole foot is on the ground. When landing on the heel (figure 3.1), the back part of the shoe will touch the ground first and then the rest of the foot slaps down, until the foot is in complete contact with the ground.

Figure 3.1 Heel-strike touchdown.

Supporting

The support phase (figure 3.2) is brief and occurs when the whole foot is on the ground and when the force of the landing is transmitted up through the knee and hip.

Pulling

In the heel strike, especially if it is front of the center of gravity, you actually pull your body over your leg and leave the ground off all your toes. Pulling your body over your leg after the interruption of the forward movement caused by the braking action of overstriding is not the most effective propulsive force to use. If you plant your foot under the center of gravity, the pulling motion is reduced, and you can push off more efficiently (figure 3.3).

Figure 3.2   Heel-strike supporting phase.

Figure 3.3   Heel-strike pulling phase.

Preparing for Forefoot Strike

If you would like to become a midfoot or forefoot striker, start by slowly building up the strength in the muscles and ligaments of your feet, especially the arch. You can do this by mastering three simple exercises: walking, squatting, and jumping. Each provides specific benefits and all promote sensory feedback and relaxation.

WALKING EXERCISE

Aim for a balanced, upright posture. Your ears should be above your shoulders, not in front of or behind them. Your shoulders should be over your hips. Your hips should be over your knees. And your knees should be over your ankles during the support phase. It would be helpful if you could do this barefoot on grass or a track. While walking you will probably land on your heels, but that's OK because you'll work on a forefoot plant in the other exercises. You are trying to achieve an upright, relaxed posture. Think of the big toe touching the ground last, just as you push off. You could also try putting a light book on your head when you walk. You'll know you're making progress when the book remains on your head longer. Five to ten minutes is a sufficient time for this walk.

SQUATTING EXERCISE

When you squat, keep your whole foot on the ground, especially your heels. Too many people doing squats lift their heels and lose the major benefit of the squat, ankle flexibility. The most efficient way to squat is to push your hips back like you are sitting down, keep your chest and head up, and your feet shoulder-width apart. Lower as far as you can or until your thighs are parallel to the floor, and keep your heels on the floor. You should feel the weight through your heels and then the forefoot. This may be difficult, so be patient. You can hold on to something for support to help with balance at first. You should also do this barefoot and for a total of 15 to 20 repetitions in one or two sets. This exercise will help stimulate the sensory feedback from the feet to the brain.

JUMPING EXERCISE

Jumping improves posture, relaxation, and sensory feedback. When you land, make sure your ears, shoulders, hips, knees, and ankles are all in line and then let yourself sink softly and bend slightly in your knees. You don't have to jump high; just make sure you land on the balls of your feet before your heels hit the ground and keep the knees relaxed. This is done barefoot and for a total of 20 to 30 repetitions in one or two sets.

Forefoot Strike

Both the forefoot strike and the midfoot strike depart in significant ways from the heel strike. And although the forefoot strike is different from the midfoot strike, they are similar enough that I will discuss only the forefoot strike in this section.

Landing

This phase includes the moment the forefoot touches down until the whole foot is on the ground. Land toward the outside of the foot at about the middle of the foot (figure 3.4a). Then roll inward onto the full ball of the foot (figure 3.4b) and then back to the heel.

Figure 3.4 Forefoot-strike landing phase: (a) Touching down, (b) rolling inward, and shifting back toward heel.

Supporting

This is the brief period when you make the transition from the landing to the pushing phase. The whole foot is on the ground under your center of gravity just after the heel has touched down. The knee is slightly bent (figure 3.5).

Figure 3.5 Supporting phase: The entire foot is on the ground, and the knee is slightly bent.

The forefoot strike takes place below the center of gravity, which can be loosely thought of as the area below the belly button. If the foot plants in front of the center of gravity, you tend to break your rhythm and must *pull* your body over the center of gravity rather than *push* it through the center of gravity. If the strike takes place behind the center of gravity, you tend to lean forward and you get a weaker push-off.

Pushing

The initial part of the drive phase allows your pelvis to rotate backward, called hip extension, while your foot is still on the ground. As your leg extends backward, the foot and lower leg muscles continue to build up elastic force, and as you roll forward on your foot toward the big toe, the power is released and pushes the body forward and up (figure 3.6). The big toe is the last part of the foot to leave the ground. A key is to leave the foot behind you, which means keep the foot on the ground as long as you naturally can.

Figure 3.6 Drive phase: Rolling forward onto the forefoot and pushing the body forward and up.

Pushing off provides greater force and efficiency than pulling through. Landing with your hips over your foot, with the knee relaxed and slightly bent, enables the body to maximize the forward roll on the foot and the push-off from the big toe.

As speed increases, the landing changes slightly by touching down closer to the forefoot. In sprinting (200 meters or less) you touch down on the ball of the foot in a line parallel to the little toe (figure 3.7). But you still roll back to the heel to get the most from your push-off.

Figure 3.7   Sprinting touchdown.

Preparing for the Barefoot Strike

Some of you might want to consider running barefoot. Start by walking in minimalist shoes (to ease the transition) or walking barefoot. When you think you are ready to safely run barefoot, begin doing so for a short time or distance. And start on a smooth, clean surface. If you're on a track, one or two laps is a reasonable starting distance. If you can't find an appropriate artificial-surface track, look for another artificial surface, such as an athletic field. The surface should be smooth and as clean as possible.

Increase the distance gradually. How quickly you can increase depends on your age and running background. If you are a beginning runner, you should proceed slowly into barefoot running. Start with about 2 minutes of barefoot walking. Then gradually add time—1 minute every two weeks—until you can walk and run barefoot for 12 minutes. Slowly increase the ratio of easy running to walking until you can jog barefoot for 12 minutes. It is always better to be too conservative than too aggressive. After all, you want running to last a lifetime.

If you are a more experienced runner, you can build your transition to barefoot running by proceeding slowly, beginning with 4 minutes and increasing by no more than two minutes per week. Incorporate barefoot running into your training routine. For instance, if you have a 40-minute run scheduled, run for 28 minutes and follow that with a 12-minute barefoot walk and jog.

The transition has two goals. One is to thicken the skin on the feet and develop calluses, especially near the ball of the foot. The second is to allow your body to adjust from a heel strike to the forefoot strike. Have patience. Four to six months is a relatively small amount of time to invest in fine-tuning your approach to a potentially lifelong activity. This is a good time to remember that less is often better than more.

If it is cold outside and your feet are cold, don't run outdoors. If you have any kind of foot problem, check with a physician before you try running barefoot or in minimalist shoes. If you experience pain, especially in the arches, back off and let the body heal. Running in chest-deep water in a pool where you can practice forefoot striking is a good substitute during this period. Your body will experience less impact, and the water will provide a gentle massage that promotes recovery. In fact, beginning the transition to barefoot running in the water is a great option for everyone!

Ankles

Your ankles should remain flexible during the stride. The more rigid they are, the more force your body will experience as your foot contacts the ground. When your foot strikes the ground during forefoot running, your ankle should be plantar flexed (toes pointed down) at an angle greater than 90 degrees. When your heel strikes first, the ankle is dorsiflexed (toes point up) and the angle is less than 90 degrees. This makes it more likely your foot will slap down when heel striking.

During the support phase of the stride, the ankle should be dorsiflexed (figure 3.8a). This means the top of the foot is angled toward the body. From this position the ankle can release elasticity and power as the toes push against the ground to achieve plantar flexion in the push phase (figure 3.8b). If you are a heel striker, the angle at the ankle rarely is less than 90 degrees and therefore much of the elastic force is lost.

Figure 3.8 The ankle (a) dorsiflexes during the support phase, then (b) explosively shifts to plantar flexion during the push phase.

Knees

The knee should be slightly bent and relaxed when you land and just a little in front of your center of gravity. It remains slightly bent during the support phase (figure 3.9). As the body moves over the knee, it begins to straighten and is straight immediately before the big toe leaves the ground (figure 3.10). As the body goes through the drive phase, the other knee swings forward with the heel approaching the butt (figure 3.11). The heel reaches closer to the butt as speed increases. Allowing the knee to swing forward rather than forcing it forward allows the hip extensor muscles, especially the gluteal muscles, to complete their work of pulling the knee down and back without interference. The knee will swing high enough if it is relaxed and then the quadriceps can extend the lower leg and prepare for landing (figure 3.12). The

Figure 3.9 Support phase: knee is slightly bent.

Figure 3.10 Straight knee immediately before big toe leaves the ground.

Figure 3.11 The knee swings forward as the heel approaches the butt.

Figure 3.12 Lower-leg extension in preparation for landing.

relaxed, swinging action of the knee ensures the foot is high enough off the ground. If you sense your foot is too low, it may be because your knee is too low. Picturing yourself trying to spring over a small obstacle should help you swing your leg at the right height. As speed increases, the height of your swing should increase (figure 3.13).

Figure 3.13 Higher knee swing associated with faster running.

Pelvis and Shoulders

The pelvic area, which provides the core of your running strength, needs to provide the stability and flexibility for smooth, cyclical leg movements at the hip joint. From the landing phase to the drive phase, your legs should continue to roll over the ground like a wheel. Watch a cheetah: By pawing back, it rolls over the ground.

The pelvic area, with the belly button as a guide, should face the direction you want to move. There should be no horizontal or twisting movement of the belly button. It will probably move vertically, but only slightly. You want to roll, not bounce. As one leg goes back with the foot on the ground, the pelvic area should have the flexibility to rotate slightly back with the leg (figure 3.14a).

Figure 3.14 (a) The hip rotates slightly backward with the leg, and (b) the shoulders stay parallel to the ground and over the hips.

The shoulders, like the pelvis, act as a stabile foundation, but this time for the arms. The shoulders provide a platform around which the arms swing. The shoulders of some runners sway back and forth or even dip. These extraneous movements decrease efficiency because they direct body movement laterally rather than forward. Shoulders should remain parallel to the ground and over the hips (figure 3.14b).

Arms

The arms and legs swing in rhythm with each other. Moving the arms faster and with a larger arc helps you pick up the pace. When you swing your arms, make sure the elbows stay close to your body and low. Elevated elbows that stick out from your body force the shoulders to sway and the body to twist.

Also make sure the angle at your elbow changes during your arm swing. When your arm is in front of the body, the elbow angle is about 45 degrees (figure 3.15a). The hand should never cross the centerline of the body and should rarely rise higher than midsternum. When your elbow is next to your body, the angle should be a little more than 90 degrees (figure 3.15b). And as it moves behind the body it may open to 150 degrees (figure 3.15c).

Rigid elbows produce swaying, twisting, loss of power, and loss of balance. The arm gets its power from the motion at elbow level. Try hammering a nail with a stiff elbow, and then let the angle constantly change and notice how much more force you generate.

The wrist should be fixed in a line with the forearm. Bending it one way or the other disrupts the path of the arm swing.

Figure 3.15 During the arm swing, the angle of the elbow changes from (a) 45 degrees when in front of the body, (b) to 90 degrees when next to the body, and (c) opens up to as much as 150 degrees when behind the body.

The hand controls the tension in the arm and shoulder. It should remain relaxed. See what happens when you tightly clench your fists. The tightness works its way all the way to the shoulder. The fingers can help ensure that the hand, and as a result, the arm and shoulder remain relaxed. The fingers should make a loose, relaxed fist. Pretend you are gently holding a beautiful feather between the thumb and both the index and middle fingers. It is delicate, and you don't want to drop or crush it (figure 3.16).

Figure 3.16 Hands are loose, and the fingers are lightly curled.

Head

The head should stay in line with the shoulders. If you dropped a plumb line from your ear, the line would go through the center of the shoulder joint, the hip joint, and the knee and ankle joints during the support phase (figure 3.17). Like the fingers, the facial muscles spread tension or relaxation to other areas; in this case the neck, upper back, and shoulders—so keep them loose and soft. The jaw should be relaxed and slightly open. A clenched jaw causes the muscles in the neck and upper back to tighten.

Figure 3.17 The head should be aligned with the belly button, and the face and jaw should be free of tension.

Breathing

Inhale through the nose and mouth. And as you inhale, achieve as much lung volume as possible by expanding your abdomen and ribs, which pushes the diaphragm down and expands the lungs. When you exhale, the abdomen and ribs should move back in, decreasing the lung volume.

When you go out for a run, periodically say to yourself, "For the next block. I'm going to practice belly breathing." I had to spend an entire winter practicing belly breathing, but when I got the hang of it, it made my runs—especially the ends of hard runs—easier.

Use figure 3.18 to check your running form.

Drills to Improve Your Form

Nearly everyone can improve some aspect of their running form. Runners can use exercises to refine and improve their form. Here are four drills to develop efficient running form.

Figure 3.18 Running Form Checklist

☐ The body is tall, not bent.

☐ The head is over the body, not bowed forward or tilted back. The jaw is relaxed.

☐ The shoulders, elbows, and fingers are relaxed. And the angle at the elbow changes during the arm swing.

☐ The belly button at the center of gravity faces forward.

☐ The legs cycle under the hip joint, which extends backward as the leg moves back.

☐ The knee is straight only at the end of the drive phase.

☐ During both heel striking and the forefoot striking, the foot lands under the center of gravity.

☐ When landing on the forefoot, the foot strikes the ground at the middle of the outside of the sole and rolls in and back.

☐ During both heel striking and forefoot striking, the foot "stays behind" as the center of gravity moves forward, and when it leaves the ground, the last part to push off is the big toe.

☐ The body maintains a good posture while remaining *relaxed* in the following areas:

Loose neck and face muscles	Loose, but not floppy, wrists
Loose, slightly open jaw	Unclenched fist
Shoulders back	Curled, relaxed fingers
Elbow position that changes during arm swing	

There is one more thing to remember: breathe.

SKIPPING

This drill consists of the skipping you did when you were young. It's fun, it encourages balanced body alignment, and it enhances relaxation. It also prepares you for what Arthur Lydiard, the legendary coach from New Zealand, called springing.

SPRINGING

Just as the name implies, you spring into the air off of the drive leg. The lead leg bends as the knee rises so that the thigh is parallel to the ground (a). When you land on the lead leg, it bends slightly to absorb the landing (b). Then that leg becomes the driving leg and you spring again. Instead of trying to move horizontally, try to move both forward and up. Emphasize extending the drive leg and pushing strongly off the toes. This drill develops the calf, ankle, and arch. If you have not done this type of drill before, start slowly and easily after you are comfortable skipping.

BUTT FLICK

Raise your heel to your butt by using the hamstrings to raise the lower legs and feet toward the butt and use the hip flexors to lift your knees like you do when running. You may be familiar with the butt kick, in which you only use your hamstrings to raise the lower leg and heel toward the butt behind you instead of under you. This is not what you do in running. The flick helps establish the leg recovery pattern that occurs after the drive.

UPHILL RUNNING

Repeated, short segments of uphill running get you thinking about your alignment and mechanics. You can start with 4 or 5 repeats of about 25 to 50 meters on a moderate hill. Hill repeats enhance leg extension and encourage landing on the ball of the foot.

4

Challenge and Adaptation

I've been fortunate to speak in front of audiences all over the world. Coaches and athletes, no matter where they're from, are always looking for ways to train smarter. During these speaking engagements I ask the same question. European coaches know the answer. In the United Sates, however, I have only gotten the right answer once, in a clinic I gave at a state penitentiary. An older inmate knew the answer. Now I'm going to share the question with you because every athlete should know the answer. It is that important. Who is Dr. Hans Selye?

Hans Selye developed the most important training theory ever . . . period. Let's back up a little.

Overtraining is a big problem. A good work ethic is important, but sometimes it takes more courage and intelligence to rest rather than to push. Too many people think that poor workouts or races are a result of not working hard enough when, in fact, their poor performance is a result of overworking. This chapter presents the single most important concept for successful training.

Training, of course, includes running, but is not limited to it. Training also requires physical, mental, and emotional effort. And to train and race successfully, you must not only challenge the body but also allow recovery from those challenges.

Selye's General Adaptation Syndrome

Challenges are the demands you place on the resources of the body. Challenges can be physical, mental, and emotional. The level of the challenge your body perceives depends on your resources.

Resources in this sense are defined as the current condition of the 12 systems of your body. Although they are all equally important, the cardiovascular, respiratory, and muscular are the more important systems for runners. These systems respond to challenge by providing structure, response, energy, and movement. The goal of a well-planned training program is to increase your body's resources. You use up your resources when meeting a challenge and rebuild and improve them during recovery from the challenge.

Recovery is the absence of challenge and the active, conscious restoration of resources. During recovery adaptation takes place.

Adaptation is the improvement of resources. Adaptation is stimulated by challenge, but it only occurs during recovery. Too much challenge depletes your resources, and too much recovery limits improvement to your resources. An intelligent balance between challenge and recovery allows your resources to adapt to the challenges of training.

Stress

Adapting to challenge is the key to improvement. To appreciate the adaptation process it helps to know about Selye and his theory of general adaptation syndrome. His landmark book, *The Stress of Life* (1956, New York: McGraw-Hill) summarizes his research on adaptation.

In the early 1930s, Selye was a medical student in Austria. He noticed that several symptoms, such as achy joints, a sore throat, or a low-grade fever, were often precursors to other more serious problems. He wanted to know what "just being a little sick" meant. Could the symptoms be prevented? If so, how? Was treatment possible at this stage?

He chose as his life's work to investigate the body's response to prolonged challenge and used a word we are all familiar with to describe this phenomenon: *stress*. Although the word *stress* had been used before, Selye was the first to use it in a biological context. He found that serious, hidden changes were associated with too much challenge. He found three areas of the body that responded to too much stress in a negative manner: the adrenal glands, the lymph system, and the digestive system. Researchers have expanded Selye's list of affected areas to include the pituitary gland, pancreas, liver, kidney, and sex hormones. Table 4.1 lists stress-related problems.

Table 4.1 Problems Associated With Excessive Stress

Decreases	Increases
Amino acid uptake	Protein breakdown
Muscle repair	Infections
White blood cells	Ulcers
Iron stores	Blood pressure
Immune response	Cortisol
Adrenalin stores	Mood disruption
Testosterone levels	

Alarm Stage

Selye divided the body's reaction to challenge into three stages: alarm, adaptation, and exhaustion. The alarm stage consists of two parts. During the first part of this stage, the body encounters a challenge. Nerve and hormonal messages mobilize resources to meet the challenge and are depleted. During the second part of the alarm stage—recovery—the challenge is removed and resources are restored. The alarm stage normally lasts 24 to 72 hours. But it can last longer depending on the nature of the challenge. For example, after a marathon, the recovery stage may take four weeks. Figure 4.1 illustrates the components of the general adaptation syndrome.

Selye said this about the alarm stage, "In the Alarm Stage the body experiences a drain on energy, structural and raw material reserves. It also experiences significant cellular destruction. No organism can maintain this stage continuously. It either has to resist stressors or die. In most cases it resists and adapts." (From Selye's book, *The Stress of Life*, published in 1956 by McGraw-Hill)

The recovery portion of the alarm stage builds up resources. If the proper food, rest, sleep, and relaxation are provided, the resources will be restored and the body can resist the stressors and adapt.

Adaptation Stage

When the alarm stage is repeated intelligently and consistently—balancing challenge with enough recovery—the system resources in the body will increase. These intelligently repeated alarm stages become the adaptation stage. In this stage, which can last up to 11 months, resources increase noticeably and performance and health improve. Refer to figure 4.1, which

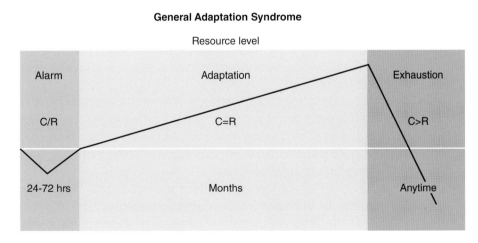

Figure 4.1   Alarm stage; adaptation stage; exhaustion stage.

shows the resource levels increasing over several months when challenge and recovery are balanced.

Table 4.2 shows some of the resources that improve by balancing challenge and recovery. As you can see, the well-planned challenge and recovery affects a wide range of functions that lead to improved running performance.

Table 4.2   Resource Improvement Associated With Balanced Challenge and Recovery

Structural	Oxygen transport	Metabolic
Stronger bones	Increased heart volume	Increased aerobic enzymes
Stronger ligaments	Increased heart vascularity	Increased anaerobic enzymes
Stronger tendons	Increased heart contractile force	Increased muscle ATP
Cartilage compressibility	Increased vagus control of heart rate, which slows down the resting heart rate.	Increased muscle DNA
Increased muscle protein	Increased blood volume	Increased muscle potassium
Decreased neural inhibition	Increased muscle capillaries	Increased glycogen storage

Exhaustion Stage

If the challenge is too severe or applied over too long a time, if recovery is insufficient, or if additional life challenges are added, adaptation and enthusiasm will be replaced by injury, illness, boredom, and fatigue. This is Selye's third stage: exhaustion. During the exhaustion stage, resource levels drop toward or below their original levels. Refer to figure 4.1, which shows what happens when challenges are greater than recovery.

The onset of the exhaustion stage is accompanied by a degeneration of adrenal gland function. The adrenal glands are located on top of each kidney. Among other things, they help the body meet challenges by releasing adrenalin into the blood stream where it interacts with various systems to supercharge the body.

When adrenal function is impaired, the body cannot fully respond to challenges. In training it means that you can't reach normal levels of training, and you feel more tired rather than invigorated. In racing it means that you can maintain your goal pace for a while, but when it comes time to finish the race, you can't switch to a faster gear.

Selye found that the adrenal glands reflect the stages of his general adaptation syndrome. In the alarm and adaptation stages, they are firm, the proper size, and are filled with vitamin C. In the exhaustion stage, they become swollen, lose vitamin C, and gain fat droplets. If the exhaustion stage lasts too long, the adrenal glands become small and hard and almost completely lose their ability to release adrenalin into the body.

It is easy to recognize the clues that you might be experiencing the onset of the exhaustion stage. However, when runners observe these signs of overtraining, many of them misinterpret their cause and react by increasing the challenge. The *only* solution is to reduce or remove the challenge. If in doubt, *rest*. Table 4.3 lists clues that indicate you might be overtraining.

Table 4.3 Symptoms of the Exhaustion Stage

Challenges seem more difficult
Psyching up seems more difficult
Hitting goal times seems more difficult
Irritation increases
Disinterest in surroundings increases
Abnormal weight loss occurs
Appetite is poor
Sleep quality is poor
Facial skin color and texture are poor
Fever blisters and canker sores appear
Muscle and joint soreness increase
Exercise, resting, and morning heart rate increase

Striking the Right Balance

Both Arthur Lydiard (accomplished runner and legendary Olympic coach from New Zealand) and Bill Bowerman (legendary U.S. Olympic coach and longtime coach at the University of Oregon)—both early promoters of running for fitness—agreed that although it is best to be properly trained, it is much better to be undertrained than overtrained. It is better to be somewhere in the adaptation stage, even if it is not at the peak, than to be in the exhaustion stage as you approach a big race.

Although both knew that training should not always be easy, they advised runners to "train, don't strain." And they believed that smart runners enjoy training because they are confident enough to understand that progress does not require continually testing themselves. When it's time for the target race, healthy, fully-functioning adrenal glands will allow runners to get the most from their training and from themselves.

At least once a year you should take a month off from serious training, speed work, and racing. Instead, you should walk or participate in other recreational activities: recreation = *re-creation*. During your break, your resource levels will decrease but not all the way to your starting level. And you should start your next racing season with a resource level higher than you started the previous season.

Herb Lindsay's training offers a good look at the three stages of the body's reaction to challenge. Lindsay was a U.S. road racing athlete of the year in the early 1980s. The workouts during Lindsay's alarm stages were challenging but doable. He alternated harder days with easy days and raced every 12 weeks. Unless the race was a goal race, he made sure the pace and competition were not excessive. Then he took one week off. So in a year, the total time he spent participating in recreational activities equaled a month. Each time he started a new training sequence, his starting level was higher than his previous starting level, so by the time he reached his goal race, he was at a higher level of fitness.

His agent suggested that he could make more money if he raced more often. He followed the agent's advice and by the end of the next year he was deep in Selye's exhaustion stage. He did not win a race that year, was far from being road racer of the year, and soon thereafter decided to retire.

In sharp contrast to Lindsay's experience is Shelly Steely's preparation for the U.S. Olympic Trials in 1992. Three weeks before the trials, she ran a very poor 3,000 meters in San Jose. She told me she felt she was a little tired. As her coach, I was not surprised at her race result because some of her training in the previous two weeks had been a little off. Most athletes and coaches facing that situation believe that the answer is to train harder. What I had Shelly do instead, and she bought into it, was to put her running shoes away and *knit* instead of train for the next 10 days. She set a personal best in the 3,000 finals in New Orleans and made the Olympic team.

Daily Resource Recovery

5

Chapter 4 emphasizes the importance of balancing challenge with recovery. Often coaches and athletes either don't discuss recovery or address it cursorily, almost as an afterthought. However, to improve performance, recovery is as important as challenge, and it demands as much planning and discipline as challenge. If you do not respect recovery, you cannot expect to improve your resources.

The goal of recovery is to restore the resources used to meet the challenge. If both challenge and recovery are undertaken properly, the resources will not only return to previous levels, but also will exceed them. You will develop the resources that will allow you to become stronger and faster and have greater endurance. You will experience genuine adaptation.

Nutrition

Many factors affect recovery, but nutrition is a good place to begin. If you do not provide the body with the raw materials required to rebuild, recovery cannot take place. The better the food and the more timely its consumption, the better the recovery. We address pre- and postworkout nutrition in part II of the book, so here we'll focus on general nutrition.

Not All Foods Are Created Equal

In 1993, Roy Vartabedian, PhD, who worked at the Cooper Clinic in Dallas, Texas, published a book called *Nutripoints*, which is in its fifth edition. In it he evaluates many foods and assigns each a single point value. His ratings eliminate the need to examine the foods to determine their makeup—carbohydrate, protein, fat, mineral, vitamins, and fiber. Instead, you can simply look at the overall point value, which has been calculated based on each food's makeup. Initially, values were difficult to interpret because different quantities of the food were compared—ounces, cups, tablespoons—making it difficult to compare equal quantities of the food. In 1993, I normalized the servings, based on the same quantity of food, so that more useful comparisons could be made.

Another problem solved by this rating system is being able to tell at a glance which food is best in each food category. Normalizing the scores on a 10-point scale makes it easier to position the foods on the food ladder. The top score in each food group is 10.

In this system, foods receive a positive or a negative score. Foods with a positive score promote good health and help you restore your resources. And while foods that receive a negative score provide calories, they may actually detract from your overall ability to replenish and recover. Because they lack nutrients and require more from the body's resources than they provide, they offer little beyond empty calories. And some even contain chemicals (for example, preservatives) that the body doesn't need. These nutrient-free foods are often expensive in terms of performance, health, and money. That doesn't mean you can't eat them. It just means you should limit them and not use them as substitutes for real food.

Foods are commonly divided into groups based on the particular type of nutrition they provide. Because your body requires different amounts of food from each group, you should not compare values from different groups. Nor should you compensate for consistently missing one food group by eating more from another food group. Each group provides specific nutrients. Each food group is necessary. Tables 5.1 and 5.2 list the top 10 positive foods in each group and the bottom 5 negative foods in each group.

Table 5.1 Nutripoint Values for Vegetables, Fruits, and Grains

Plus	Vegetables	Fruits	Grains
10	Brussels sprouts	Kiwi	Wheat bran
9	Carrots	Cantaloupe, or rockmelon	Wheat germ
8	Spinach	Black berries	Muesli cereal
7	Broccoli	Raspberries	Shredded-wheat cereal
6	Asparagus	Apricots	Oatmeal
5	Cauliflower	Figs	Mixed-grain cereal
4	Cabbage	Strawberries	Wild rice
3	Mushrooms	Prunes	Whole-wheat pasta
2	Squash	Dates	Brown rice
1	Tomatoes	Raisins	Whole-grain pasta
Minus			
-5	Hash browns	Jam	Fast-food pastry
-4	French fries	Sherbet	Doughnut
-3	Cup of canned soup	Fruit drink	Twinkie
-2	Potato chips	Pie	Fast-food french toast
-1	Onion rings	Fruit in syrup	Commercial cookies, or biscuits

Table 5.2 Nutripoint Values for Legumes, Dairy Products, and Meats

Plus	Legumes	Dairy	Meats
10	Sunflower seeds	Nonfat dry milk	Tuna*
9	Kidney beans	Nonfat milk	Organic beef liver
8	Garbanzo beans	Cottage cheese	Salmon
7	Navy beans	Yogurt	Swordfish
6	Peas	Ovaltine	Organic liverwurst
5	Lima beans	2% milk	Halibut
4	Pinto beans	Whole milk	Skinless turkey
3	Walnuts	Chocolate milk	Skinless chicken
2	Roasted soy beans	Milkshake	Flounder
1	Roasted pumpkin seeds	Swiss cheese	Red Snapper
Minus			
-5	Peanut brittle	Whipped cream	Pepperoni
-4	Peanut butter cup	Margarine	Hot dog
-3	Chocolate-covered peanuts	Cheese spread	Pork sausage patty
-2	Fast-food burritos	Fast-food milkshake	Fast-food fried chicken
-1	Oil-roasted pecans	Fast-food breakfast sandwich	Fast-food cheeseburger

*Tuna may contain mercury because it is at the top of the food chain. The value does not account for mercury.

Another advantage of this rating system and eating from each food group is that if you follow the handful guidelines, you automatically balance your consumption of calories, carbohydrate, protein, fat, minerals, vitamins, and fiber. You don't have to count the separate nutrients or count calories.

Table 5.3 lists not only the food groups you should choose your foods from, but also suggests how many servings, measured as a handful, of food from each group you should eat per day. These servings are for a runner weighing about 155 pounds (70 kg). If you weigh significantly more than

Table 5.3 Suggested Number of Handfuls per Food Group

Food group	Handfuls for 155-lb (70 kg) runner
Water	8-12
Vegetables	6-7
Fruits	4-5
Grains	3-4
Legumes	1-2
Dairy	2-3
Meats	1-2
Junk food and fast food	0-3

this, add one serving to each category. If you weigh significantly less than this, subtract one serving. Add or subtract one handful for every 25 pounds greater or less than 155. Experiment from this baseline because your nutrient intake is variable depending on several factors, including intensity and duration of your training. The normalized serving size chosen was the handful, which has been adopted by many nutritionists. The handful works well in a practical sense because it is a readily available measuring tool: what you can comfortably hold in your hand is a handful. Also, a reasonably accurate assumption can be made that larger people require more food and this will usually be compensated for by larger hands.

Water is listed as the first food group. Getting enough water is crucial because it is the environment in which your cells must live. If you drink insufficient amounts of water, you create an increasingly alien environment for your cells.

When using this table, consider juice equal to the actual food value if the skin of the fruit is kept on. For example, a cup of juice made from the whole fruit or vegetable is almost the same as a handful of fruits or vegetables. Dried food can be equal to almost twice the food value. A handful of dried apples is almost the same as two apples. But remember, drink even more water if you eat a lot of dried fruit. If water is added to food such as rice or dry milk and then cooked, the water plus the food equals the serving size. Adding water to cook rice to make a cup (handful) of rice gives you one serving.

Get More From Your Food

When you shop for or prepare your food remember that the food value can be increased or decreased by how the food is grown, processed, and prepared. When shopping, think about the value the food has to offer.

- How food is grown: Organic is better than pesticide free, which is better than food grown on a corporate farm.
- How food is processed: Fresh is better than frozen, which is better than canned, which is better than processed (ingredients added or deleted).
- How food is prepared: Fresh is better than steamed, which is better than boiled, which is better than baked, which is better than broiled, which is better than fried.
- Food value: Advertisers program you to think in terms of money per pound. Instead, determine money per nutrient.

An effective way to begin to change your diet is through what I call the Big Day Diet. Try to eat healthily six days each week. On the seventh day, whichever day you choose, you get a big day. On the big day you can eat whatever you want and as much of it as you want. This gives you permission to eat foods you really like but may not be great for you. It also helps you control the amount of nutrient-free food you eat. It doesn't take long before you fail to notice the big day. This means your body is adjusting to a proper diet and no longer craves the high levels of sugar, salt, and saturated fat in junk food and fast food. In fact, if you suddenly eat a meal that is high in fat, sugar, or salt you might even feel somewhat ill, as I did after eating a tasty cut of fatty beef in a popular New York restaurant!

Start Your Day With Breakfast

Eat breakfast! As soon as your day begins you should provide your body with nourishment. Getting good food into your body soon after you wake up is crucial because you have been on an eight-hour fast. So you need to break . . . fast. Your body requires a supply of raw materials. If it doesn't get them, two things occur. First, your body will perceive that you are starving, and it will tend to store fat for a "rainy day." Second, it will then use glucose, which has been used most of the night to feed the brain. Without breakfast, your glucose reserves will be depleted further, leaving less available for an upcoming workout. By skipping breakfast you conserve fat and deplete glucose energy stores. In addition, a good breakfast will increase your metabolic rate, making it easier for you to maintain an efficient muscle-to-fat ratio. Indeed, one of the reasons for a short, easy morning run is to help jump-start your metabolism.

If you eat a fast-food or junk-food breakfast, you will experience a sugar high. Soon afterward, you will experience a low, because insulin has been released to maintain proper blood sugar levels. It does this by removing excess glucose and storing it as fat. Soon you feel like you are hungry for something sweet, and the vicious cycle starts again.

Drinking caffeinated beverages at breakfast gives you a boost by releasing adrenalin. However, this is not advantageous. Releasing adrenalin when there is no fight-or-flight situation wastes adrenalin. Using caffeine daily also nullifies its effect if you choose to drink a moderate amount of coffee before a competition.

Eating a well-balanced breakfast does your body a big favor and aids recovery. When you wake up you should know that before the day's end you will provide your body with the proper type and amount of nutrients it needs to supply energy and resources for training and for recovery from training. You should devote part of the day to making sure you fulfill your nutritional goals as well as workout goals. Both daily goals are crucial to intelligent training.

Get Enough Calories

Finally, during heavy, consistent training you may need more calories. If you know you will consume a proper diet by the end of the day and you still feel hungry after eating nutritious food, it is OK to eat foods with a high caloric content, such as cookies (or biscuits), chocolate, and ice cream. As an athlete, you will convert more calories than the average person and may need some of those empty calories to restock glucose supplies. But don't eat the empty-calorie foods as a substitute for nutritious foods. Eat them in addition to the nutritious foods. Perhaps a better choice when you are hungry is to drink a glass of chocolate milk. It is also beneficial to eat smaller meals more often than to eat three traditional larger meals a day. You might consider three balanced meals and two balanced snacks a day.

Consider Dietary Supplements

A healthy diet should provide you with appropriate levels of proper nutrients. However, as a runner, you will likely push your body well past where most people venture. While the government publishes minimum daily requirements and recommended daily requirements, it does not publish optimum daily requirements. Therefore, to ensure that your body gets enough of the nutrients that support training, it is advisable to augment a proper diet with supplements, especially if you log a lot of mileage.

Of the many claims about the value of various supplements, some are probably true. If you were to examine each claim in great detail, however, it could become your life's work. Therefore, we must rely on scientific literature and experience. With that in mind and with the caveat that this is a short list, table 5.4 lists supplements to consider. The substances listed in the first column are associated with the benefits listed in the second. Although research has yet to prove that these supplements yield the alleged benefits in all cases, many runners swear by them. Given that these substances have not been shown to be harmful when taken in reasonable quantities, the potential benefits seem to outweigh the risks. The athletes I coached generally found these supplements helpful, as do I to this day.

Except for vitamin C, follow the dosage recommendations printed on the bottle. An optimal dose of vitamin C is typically 3,000 to 6,000 milligrams per day. In my experience, better-quality supplements are available at health food or specialty vitamin stores than at chain outlets, grocery stores, or drugstores.

Table 5.4 Potentially Helpful Supplements

Supplement	Benefit
Vitamin C	Prevents illness, speeds healing of injury, promotes proper function of adrenal gland
Multivitamin	Ensures sufficient nutrient consumption
Vitamin D	Boosts immune system, promotes bone and muscle health
Omega-3 fatty acids	Boosts immune system, regulates blood pressure
Organic desiccated liver	Provides iron for red blood cells

Sleep and Relaxation

Another factor that affects recovery is giving your body enough time and the right conditions to recover from a challenge. Recovery requires that you avoid challenges for a while and place yourself in an environment that lets your body focus on recovering. Sleep is the best way to do this.

During sleep, restoration is the goal. Most people need seven to eight hours of sleep a night. However, when I conducted a study with Olympic-caliber runners, I found effective sleep hours ranged from 6:40 to 9:20. Sleep is most effective when it has a regular place in your 24-hour cycle. Going to bed and getting up at the same time enhances sleep. Your body develops a rhythm within which hormones, which control body processes, are released. If these rhythms remain undisturbed, the body functions more efficiently.

Periods of relaxation are also important. Times when you free your mind from the challenges of training or other life events become important periods of restoration. Active rest, where you are moderately active but only do what you enjoy, is an example of a break your body needs to restore itself from a season of training and racing. During active rest, participate in recreational activities you can't do when you are training. Recreation is really re-creation.

You can also take minivacations that in a few minutes each day provide significant restorative benefits. Many studies support the benefits of brief, but intelligent, relaxation. Herbert Benson, a Harvard professor and physician with degrees in Western and Eastern medicine wrote a book called the *Relaxation Response* (first published by Harper Collins in 1975, with the latest edition in 2000). In it he presents relaxation techniques from around the world. He found that all the techniques had four things in common. All involved

- finding a quiet place in which to relax,
- getting in a comfortable position and closing your eyes,
- letting go of worrisome thoughts, and
- repeating a gentle sound to help decrease focus on worrisome thoughts.

His research showed that when people spent 10 minutes a day on relaxation, their pulse rate, blood pressure, and metabolism all decreased. People also stated they felt refreshed.

Weather and Traffic

Weather and traffic can cause problems for runners. Running teaches you to tune into what's going on inside yourself and it gets you out of the house, the office, and the car. Most of the time, outside is a great place to be. But sometimes you need to prepare before going comfortably and safely into the world. Dressing for the weather can help you preserve body resources so you can recover faster from setbacks and, most important, avoid illness.

Because weather won't adapt to you, you must learn to cope with it, especially on the hottest and coldest days. Most runners train on roads for the practical reason that roads are almost everywhere and nearly always accessible. But running on the road puts you in competition with the single greatest physical threat a runner faces: automobile traffic. Here are tips for dealing with the weather and traffic.

Weather

Weather conditions during your run won't necessarily remain the same throughout your run. Don't believe only what you see as you look out the window when you're preparing for a run, and don't dress based solely on what the thermometer says. Check the weather forecast and radar map and pay attention to how the clouds are moving. Over time you may learn to read the cloud movement and cloud color and make inferences about the upcoming weather. Err on the side of caution if there's a chance you'll need an extra layer or rain gear; better to return from your run with an extra item wrapped around your waist than to return chilled to the bone or soaked to the skin.

Winter days won't seem as cold once you start your run, and summer days won't feel as comfortable as they did when you set out. That's because of the 20 degrees Fahrenheit (° F) rule, which quantifies how much the exertion of running warms a runner on a cold day or makes the heat less bearable on a hot day. The rule says the perceived temperature will climb by about 20° F (10° C) as you hit your stride.

For example, a chilly 40° F (5° C) morning will feel like a pleasant 60° F (15° C). A balmy 75° F (24° C) afternoon will seem like an unpleasant 95° F (35° C). Your body has a good furnace but a bad air conditioner. It warms up nicely in cold weather, but cools down poorly on hot days.

Plan your runs with the 20° F (10° C) rule in mind. Dress for the way the temperature will feel mid-run, not the way it feels when you start. Dress in layers that can be stripped away as you get warmer. Run in the cooler hours of a summer day. If possible, save your hardest runs for the coolest parts of the day. In winter strive for the warmer hours of the day.

Hot-Weather Ratings

Search the columns at left to find the temperature and then go across to the humidity level; the point at which the values meet is the letter grade for the day. A indicates the best conditions for running and F the worst. Temperatures below 70° F (22° C) but above the point at which you feel cold all rate A grades, and those above 95° F (35° C) rate F grades at all humidity levels.

Temperature (° F)	Temperature (° C)	Percent humidity								
		20	30	40	50	60	70	80	90	100
70	20	A	A	A	A	A	A	A	B	B
75	24	A	A	A	A	A	B	B	B	C
80	26	A	A	B	B	B	B	C	C	C
85	29	B	B	C	C	C	D	D	D	F
90	32	C	C	D	D	D	F	F	F	F
95	35	D	D	F	F	F	F	F	F	F

Cold-Weather Ratings

Search the columns at left to find the temperature and then go across to the wind reading; the point at which the values meet is the letter grade for the day. A represents the best conditions for running and F the worst. Temperatures above 35° F (1° C) but below the point at which you feel hot rate A grades, and those below -10° F (-19° C) rate F grades at most wind speeds.

Temperature (° F)	Temperature (° C)	Wind speed (mph)								
		Calm	5	10	15	20	25	30	35	40
		Wind speed (m/sec)								
		Calm	2	5	7	9	11	13	15	17
35	1	A	A	A	B	B	B	C	C	C
30	-1	A	A	B	B	B	C	C	C	D
25	-3	A	B	B	B	C	C	C	D	D
20	-6	B	B	B	C	B	C	D	D	D
15	-8	B	B	C	C	C	D	D	D	F
10	-10	B	C	C	C	D	D	D	F	F
5	-12	C	C	C	D	D	D	F	F	F
0	-15	C	C	D	D	D	F	F	F	F
-5	-17	C	D	D	D	F	F	F	F	F
-10	-19	D	D	D	F	F	F	F	F	F

Don't let summer heat or winter cold keep you indoors. If you are properly dressed, you can safely train in any season. But you must consider the potential risks at either temperature extreme. Hot days carry the possibility of heat exhaustion and cold days the risk of frostbite and hypothermia. High

> continued

> *continued*

humidity makes hot days feel hotter than the actual temperature because your body can't cool as efficiently. And high winds make cold days feel colder.

Plan your running and your wardrobe using the hot-weather readings table and the cold-weather readings table. The grades in the charts go from A, a good day to F, an unsafe day.

Each person's reaction to heat and cold is different, of course, and runners develop something of a tolerance as they continue to train in various conditions and learn how best to dress for them.

Traffic

Dedicated trails and tracks are nice bonuses, but they aren't necessary for running. Almost anywhere you can walk can become a place to run. This often means taking to the roads. For your protection, follow these rules:

- Choose roads with sidewalks or wide shoulders that can function as a safety zone, and run facing oncoming traffic.
- Be aware that running the same route repeatedly can eventually cause overuse injuries if the road you routinely run on, like most, is canted. Mix up your routes so you run on different surfaces and at different angles. Never reverse directions and run with your back to traffic, however. Try running on grass, bark trails if they are available, bike paths, and even sidewalks.
- Yield the right of way, and assume that the road belongs to those in or on vehicles, including bicycles and skateboards. Also try to avoid dogs, but if you are confronted by one it is best to stop, look it in the eye, point a straight arm and finger at the dog and yell "Back!"
- If you are passing another runner or some walkers, please indicate your presence by saying, "On your right" or "On your left."
- Treat drivers courteously, and never provoke them by invading their lanes, dashing in front of them, or berating them after close calls.
- Anticipate drivers' moves by doing the thinking for them, and make eye contact with them at risky crossings.
- Stay alert by keeping your head up and eyes on the road, and fight the tendency to daydream the miles away, ignoring road conditions.
- Wear brightly colored clothing during daytime, and wear reflective items at night to make yourself more visible.
- Listen to your environment, and leave your music, talk-radio shows, and other distractions at home so you can pay attention to your surroundings.
- Not all threats on the streets are vehicular. They can also be human. Runners, especially women, may become targets of belligerent and predatory people. To protect yourself, run in places and at times that pose minimal risk, stay alert to potential threats, and carry a small spray device.

Massage

A more active recovery technique is massage. And it need not only be done when recovering from certain injuries. Massage improves blood flow, which improves delivery of nutrients to cells and removal of waste products from the cells. It lengthens muscle fibers by reducing involuntary contractions. Both the Institute for Integrative Healthcare Studies and Associated Bodywork and Massage Professionals claim that deep-tissue massage helps break up scar tissue in the muscle and promotes proper healing of the tissue and that it can help break up scar tissue associated with muscular injuries. Deep-tissue massage is also believed to help decrease scar tissue. This reduces the stress on tendons, ligaments, and joints, which helps to reduce the risk of injury.

If you have a choice, schedule the massage the day of a hard workout after the workout is complete. It should not be done the day before a hard workout or race or the day of a hard workout unless it is a very light, loosing massage. A massage once every two weeks is a minimal investment in your recovery process. Weekly massage is helpful during the last three months before an important race.

Illness Prevention

Prevention of illness is another major part of recovery. If you don't get ill, you don't have to spend valuable time and resources recovering from it. You may encounter a bug going around that will cause illness no matter what you do. However, most of the time, whether you become a host for a bug depends on you, not the bug.

During the latter part of a workout and for about two hours after it, your immune system is depressed. During this time you are more vulnerable to illness. If you adhere to the recovery suggestions regarding diet and proper rest, your chances of hosting a bug are diminished. You can adopt the following workout habits to increase your chances of remaining healthy.

- Dress properly for the workout. Wear layers of warm clothing on cool or cold days and cover your head, throat, chest, and hands—remember, you can always take clothes off, but if you don't have them, you can't put them on.
- Warm up properly and go through the workout without lag time.
- Stay within workout parameters; if in doubt do less rather than more.
- Refuel with protein, carbohydrate, and fluids soon after the workout, preferably within 30 minutes. It can also be planned to aid recovery.
- Keep warm between the completion of your workout and your post-workout shower, which you should take as soon as possible after the workout.
- Eat and drink well, and make sure to drink plenty of water.
- Go to bed at the same time each night and get enough sleep.

Recovery Indicators

When I coached at Athletics West, I conducted a 10-month study to see whether the onset of illness could be predicted. The hope was that if illness could be predicted, it could potentially be prevented. Prevention could ensure consistent training.

After tracking 30 potential recovery indicators for 10 months in 25 athletes, I compared indicators when the athletes were healthy and when the athletes were ill. The results showed that 12 of the indicators were significantly different one, two, or three days before the onset of illness compared to when the athlete was healthy.

Normal recovery indicators suggested that recovery from previous challenges—physical, mental, or emotional—had occurred and the risk of illness had been reduced. Athletes could monitor their recovery status each morning by checking these indicators and use this information to make workout decisions.

Four of the recovery indicators we identified could be measured with equipment most people already have, cost nothing to monitor, could be measured within minutes of waking up, and were as statistically significant as the other indicators that were more expensive to monitor. The four are morning heart rate, morning body weight, time to bed, and perceived hours slept.

Monitor these indicators for yourself, and try to record the results each morning. Don't become compulsive; if you miss a day don't stress over it. But because these indicators provide valuable information, do your best to make it a habit to monitor them.

As soon as you wake up, take a reclining 1-minute morning heart rate reading. You can use your watch or the stopwatch feature or heart rate monitor app on a tablet or smart phone. As soon as you get up, urinate and have a bowel movement and then weigh yourself, nude, before you eat anything. Determine when you went to bed and calculate how many hours you believe you slept.

If you record the data consistently, you will see a pattern developing that illustrates what's normal for you. After you determine an average for each indicator, after two or three weeks, you can use your daily numbers to determine whether you are at risk of becoming ill or whether you are fully recovered from illness by comparing that day's results with the average numbers.

The recovery indicators can provide valid clues about your ability to successfully complete the intended workout for the day. They can guide your decisions about when to step things up and when to cut back. Table 5.5 lists the four indicators and the values that suggest your body needs more recovery time.

What does the data mean? At Athletics West, we told athletes that if one indicator was out of the normal range they should watch for signs that the

Table 5.5 **Four Key Recovery Indicators**

Recovery indicator	Not fully recovered
Morning heart rate	10% higher than normal
Morning body weight	3% lower than normal
Time to bed	40 minutes > later than normal
Perceived hours slept	10% less than normal

day's workout felt harder than usual and should be prepared to back off. If two indicators were out of the normal range, they should definitely plan an easy day. If more than two indicators were out of the normal range, they were to take the day off. I've used these guidelines many times since, and I recommend them for anyone in any training program.

6

Fitness and the Female Runner

While men and women have far more points of commonality than difference, and despite the fact that women now compete at levels once thought unattainable and in sports once reserved for men, the reality is that men and women evolved for different purposes. The roles of estrogen and testosterone testify to this. Hormones play a major role in the differences between male and female runners. Postpuberty testosterone in men results in broader frames, a bigger upper body with a greater lung capacity, more muscle mass with larger muscle fibers, longer legs, and stronger bones, especially where the muscles attach to bone.

Postpuberty estrogen in women prepares them for child bearing. They develop wider hips and increased hip flexibility. This includes greater tail-bone mobility, a downward pelvic tilt, and a wider, more circular pelvis.

Generally speaking, women's bones are less dense, and women have less muscle mass and more essential fat than men. They also tend to have shorter legs in relation to their height and more joint mobility. This flexibility involves the anterior shoulder joints, lumbar spine, elbows, hands, and fingers.

The pelvis is composed of the sacrum, ilium, ischium, and pubic bone. After puberty, these bones fuse into one bone and support the spine and protect the organs in the abdomen. A man's pelvic cavity is narrow and heart shaped, while a woman's pelvis is open and circular to accommodate the birth of a child. A woman's pelvis protects the uterus, fallopian tubes, and ovaries.

The angle between the femur and the tibia is different for women than for men, 17 degrees versus about 13 degrees, because of women's wider pelvis. This angle, determined by the width of the pelvis, is called the Q angle (figure 6.1), and it determines the amount of working space at the anterior cruciate ligament.

The anterior cruciate ligament connects the femur and tibia and provides stability to the knee joint, preventing it from moving too far forward and

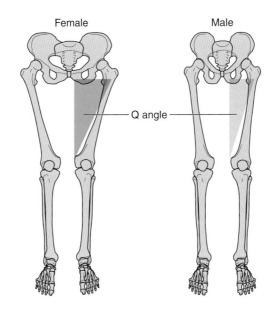

Figure 6.1 The Q angle for *(a)* women and the Q angle for *(b)* men.

rotating too far inward. As the Q angle increases, the bony projections at the end of the femur (femoral condyles) can more easily pinch the anterior cruciate ligament as the knee straightens, bends, twists, and hyperextends. Anterior knee pain in women can often be attributed to significantly larger Q angles. Pinching can cause a rupture. Women are subject to many more anterior cruciate ligament tears than men. For example, a twisting injury in a man might stretch the anterior cruciate ligament, while in women the same twist might cause a tear. Because of their higher percentage of knee injuries, women should make strengthening muscles around the knees a priority.

Muscle Mass

Estrogen limits muscle growth while testosterone encourages muscle growth. As a result, women have two-thirds less muscle mass and one-third less strength in all muscle groups than men.

Women's muscle is capable of generating the same amount of force per unit of its cross-sectional area. Although men and women possess an equal number of muscle fibers, women's muscle fibers are not as large, and therefore the cross-sectional area is not as large. Actually, pound for pound, there is not much difference in strength between the sexes. The women are not as strong because the cross-sectional area of the fibers is not as large.

Men and women respond to resistance training in the same way. However, because of hormonal differences, women develop less muscle through resistance training even though the muscle tissue composition is the same and responses to progressive overload training are the same. Both sexes gain muscle, but men gain it faster because of the difference in fiber size.

Women are relatively weaker (40 percent to 50 percent) in upper-body strength and only 20 percent to 30 percent weaker in leg strength. Actually, women's lower-body strength is relatively higher because their wider hips give them a more solid base. Squats and lunges tend to be easier for women than push-ups or pull-ups.

Body Fat

Overall, women store more fat than men. Fat accounts for about 27 percent of an average woman's weight, but only 15 percent of an average man's weight is fat.

Fat is classified as either essential or nonessential. Essential fat is important to both men and women for effective metabolism, conduction of nerve impulses, building cell structures, and protection from trauma. Sex-specific essential fat in women is stored in the breasts, under the skin, and in the pelvis, hips, thighs, and buttocks. This fat is important in child bearing.

We all know about nonessential fat. It comes from overeating and underexercising. It reduces the efficiency of body functions, especially the cardiovascular system. Greater amounts of body fat also reduce heat loss, raising the body's internal temperature. Because women sweat at higher skin and core temperatures than men, women are often less heat tolerant.

Although nonessential fat hinders endurance performance, women's higher percentage of essential fat helps them handle longer endurance events better than men. It enables women to conserve glycogen stores longer. When glycogen stores are exhausted, hydrogen ions proliferate in the production of energy, and muscle contractions become less powerful and produce pain.

$\dot{V}O_2$max

As explained in chapter 1, $\dot{V}O_2$max indicates the most oxygen you can consume during physical activity. It is measured in milliliters of oxygen consumed per kilogram of body weight per minute (ml/kg/min). It is the standard for aerobic fitness.

On average, men have higher $\dot{V}O_2$max levels and therefore greater aerobic capacity. There are several reasons for this:

- Men's hearts are larger than women's hearts.
- Men pump 16 percent more blood per beat because of the larger heart.
- Men have a larger lung capacity that can handle 25 percent more air than women's lungs.
- Men have more red blood cells and hemoglobin per cell.

Because of these differences, men have a greater ability to transport oxygen to the cells, which results in faster running times. On average, women's performance times are 15 percent to 20 percent slower than men's.

Heart Rate

The heart is a four-chambered pump. The two upper chambers (atria) receive blood from the body and the lungs. The two lower chambers (ventricles) pump blood to the lungs and the body. With each beat, blood is forced from the ventricles into arteries. Each ventricle is able to pump approximately 70 milliliters (ml) of blood per beat in men and 63 ml of blood in women.

If a man's heart pumps 70 ml per beat and beats an average of 70 beats per minute (bpm), the cardiac output, or blood pumped per beat, is 4,900 milliliters per minute (ml/min) (70 ml $\times$ 70 bpm). The output for a woman's heart beating at the same rate would be 4,400 ml/min (63 ml $\times$ 70 bpm). To pump 4,900 ml/min, the woman's heart must beat at a rate of 98 bpm. When a woman runs at the same pace as a man, not only is her heart rate higher, but also she reaches maximum heart rate sooner. The woman's heart needs to beat at a faster rate to match the output of the man's larger heart.

Men have an average resting heart rate of 70 to 72 bpm and women have an average resting heart rate of 78 to 82 bpm. World-class male athletes can have resting heart rates in the low 30s, while female world-class athletes may have a resting heart rate in the low to mid 40s.

Psychology

In my years of coaching both men and women, I have found that male and female runners often struggle with confidence but in different ways, and frequently they have learned their gender roles early.

Many of the men I coached liked to vie for the role of top dog and looked for individual praise. They often projected confidence and toughness and maybe tried to prove the coach was wrong. They were generally certain of their own prowess and maybe even resisted coaching. Men tended to depersonalize criticism and tried to deflect the criticism toward the entire team. Young men seemed more attracted to the competitive aspects of sports and were motivated by challenges to their abilities.

Among the women I coached, many felt like "we are all in this together" and were motivated by social opportunities and the unity of the team. They were often open to accepting input from others and therefore willing to learn from their coach and were comfortable trying new ideas. I also found women were more dedicated to the training regimen than their male counterparts.

Menstrual Cycle

Menstruation typically begins in the early teens and ends in the 50s. It occurs in cycles lasting 26 to 35 days. The cycle is controlled by hormones, especially estrogen and progesterone.

The cycle starts with menses that is stimulated when the released egg is not fertilized. This involves the loss of 25 to 65 milliliters of blood and fluid. It usually lasts three to five days. During this time mood can change, stressors seem more pronounced, reaction times are reduced, and the immune system is somewhat compromised. The release of estrogen and progesterone decreases during this period.

Intense training, which stimulates inflammation, may cause a decrease in iron absorption. The drop in iron and reduced iron absorption usually does not affect performance. However, if the blood loss is heavy, it might be wise to check your ferritin (protein in the cells that stores iron) levels. A drop in these levels could indicate the onset of anemia.

Menses is not the most difficult time to run, but reducing training volume might be appropriate because of the loss of red blood cells and the reduction of oxygen to the cells. Strength work is also something a woman should consider during this time.

At about day 6 of the cycle, the egg sac begins to grow and soon thereafter estrogen and growth hormone trigger the development of the egg in the ovary. The estrogen thickens the lining of the uterus as it prepares for the egg. Because the body increases glycogen uptake and storage, this is a good time for low-intensity, high-volume exercise and non-weight-bearing work such as swimming or cycling.

A fertile phase, ovulation, occurs between days 11 and 15. This is when the egg matures and is released from the ovary and travels down the fallopian tube to the uterus. Upon ovulation, estrogen levels drop and progesterone levels rise. During this period a shift back to higher intensity and lower volume might be considered. Changes in behavior, such as lack of enthusiasm, might occur and racing potential in the form of the inability to sustain effort might be affected.

If the egg is not fertilized in two or three days, the egg sac breaks apart and the egg disintegrates. This is called the luteal phase because increase in progesterone causes the luteum (lining), to break down. Many women experience water retention during at this time.

As this phase progresses, several changes occur that make running more difficult. Hormonal changes cause protein to break down more easily, resulting in lower muscular endurance. The increase in progesterone stimulates the phrenic nerve that speeds up the diaphragm, causing an excess of carbon dioxide release and a higher respiration rate. Because of this, lactate threshold decreases and anaerobic work is more difficult. There is also a drop in plasma volume. Plasma allows sweating, and if you are slower to sweat, body temperature will increase. In addition, the loss of plasma volume results in more sluggish blood flow that can increase the formation of lactate and decrease the delivery of oxygen.

Make sure you drink before and during a workout in this phase to help keep plasma volume up. Workouts that emphasize lower intensity and higher volume and include non-weight-bearing activity might help prevent protein breakdown.

The progesterone increase is followed by a drop in this hormone, causing the uterine lining to detach. During this period, mood swings might occur, stressors might seem more difficult, and reaction time might be slower because focusing is more difficult. This might be a good recovery week and a time to reduce stressors.

The detachment of the lining leads to menses and bleeding as the lining is shed from the uterus. The cycle begins again.

If the hardest time to race is the week before menstruation and week after ovulation, when is it the best time to race? While individual menstrual cycles vary, it seems that many women race best the week after menses. Others seem to race best during menses, but not the first day. On that day many women feel bloated and sometimes depressed and run very poor times. If you are interested, good times to race are days 9 through 12 and days 17 through 20.

Menstrual Irregularities

Some women have a slightly longer or shorter cycle, with slight differences in certain phases that can be tracked and then anticipated or taken into account. However, any woman's normal cycle is also subject to irregularities in response to factors such as emotional stress, illness, infection, prescription drugs, herbal preparations, and changes in exercise level. Be aware of the potential impact and be prepared to adjust your training, if necessary.

Body weight can affect the cycle. Excessive body fat can lead to abnormal bleeding patterns. Very low body weight can lead to the absence of periods, called amenorrhea, and the development of osteoporosis, muscle injuries, and reduced oxygen-carrying capacity. High calcium intake from a supplement or from legumes, dark leafy vegetables, cheese, nuts, broccoli, sardines, and salmon can help prevent osteoporosis. Iron is important in oxygen-carrying capacity and is found in liver, spinach, and some dry cereals.

Other factors that affect a woman's cycle are out of her control. These include hormonal imbalance, hormonal timing, glandular problems, and physical changes in the uterus and ovaries that accompany age or illness.

When estrogen and progesterone in the ovaries start to decrease in a woman's late 30s, osteoporosis may become more of a problem. At this time, make sure you consume enough calcium-containing foods and include strength training in your exercise routine.

Premenstrual syndrome (PMS) is associated with emotional and physical changes. Some of the most common emotional symptoms are mood swings, loss of confidence, and poor concentration. Some of the more common physical symptoms are weight gain, swollen ankles, and headaches. Drugs are available to counteract PMS in women who are particularly affected by it, but the medications often interfere with energy production at the cellular level. Increasing fruits and vegetables in the diet can help decrease the symptoms of PMS.

Some athletes use a contraceptive pill to treat PMS or to manipulate the cycle to fit into their racing schedule. Such tactics should be undertaken with caution and under a doctor's supervision because the potential side effects include fluid gain, the elimination of the vitamin B complex, decreased carbohydrate absorption, and a decrease in the manufacture of red blood cells.

Keeping a running diary and including notes on your menstrual cycle can pay dividends. Note how you feel each day when you run and see if a pattern develops.

An obvious change in the menstrual cycle is pregnancy. During this time, moderate exercise is good for both you and the baby. Running during the first trimester is safe and for most women so is running in the second trimester. Running in the third trimester is more difficult in part because the body produces a hormone called relaxin that weakens the tendons and ligaments to make the birth canal wider during birth. Running in water is a good substitute during this trimester. And remember that raising your core temperature above 101 degrees Fahrenheit (38 C) can increase the risk of birth defects. So be careful when you run in heat and stay away from hot baths or hot whirlpools.

Female Athlete Triad

The female athlete triad is a serious condition that can affect athletes that push too hard. Runners with this condition have a distorted body image and mistakenly come to believe that more running and less eating are always better, to the point of putting their health at risk. They may avoid certain types of food entirely and consider exercise and athletics more a necessity than something to enjoy.

The triad consists of amenorrhea (the absence of periods), osteoporosis (low bone density), and one or more eating disorders. It is a dangerous, potentially life-threatening, condition that calls for evaluation and treatment by medical professionals. It is often seen in younger athletes who equate extreme leanness with running fast, looking attractive, and being in control. While it is true that in some cases reducing body fat can help increase $\dot{V}O_2$max and lead to faster running times, body weight that is too low is detrimental to running performance, fitness, and overall health.

Eating disorders commonly seen in the triad are anorexia nervosa and bulimia nervosa, which result in a low overall caloric intake and low energy availability. Restricted eating combined with excessive exercise drastically reduces the energy the body can use to carry out normal functions, including a regular menstrual cycle, sufficient bone density, and basic cell maintenance.

Without treatment, the female athlete triad can progress, making treatment and recovery increasingly difficult and sometimes ultimately putting the athlete's life at risk.

Menopause

At menopause, which usually occurs in the early 50s, the ovaries shut down, you are no longer fertile, and you have no more menstrual cycles. The transition from reduced periods to no periods as the estrogen levels decrease is unpredictable and may take three to five years. Eventually, menopause is confirmed when a woman has had no periods for a year. Although about 10 percent of women seek medical help to treat side effects, menopause is a part of life, not a disease.

Many symptoms accompany the transition to menopause (perimenopause) and can last from months to several years as they gradually taper. They begin with irregular periods and lower fertility. Vaginal dryness can also occur, which can be countered with water-based lubricants and by staying sexual active. Urinary problems as the urethra and vagina lose elasticity could also occur. This can be countered by doing Kegel exercises three or four times a day.

Some women experience weight gain and a buildup of fat in the abdomen. Obesity could become a problem, but it can be countered by staying physically active and eating a well-balanced diet of unprocessed foods and consuming 200 to 400 fewer calories a day than you ate before perimenopause.

Other symptoms include hair loss and a decrease in breast size. Disturbed sleep is often associated with night sweats and hot flashes. This can be countered to some extent by exercising, reducing caffeine and alcohol, keeping rooms cooler, and wearing loose clothes.

With all these symptoms possible and being more susceptible to stress, changes in mood and depression could also become a problem. Again, exercise, rest, and a healthful diet are a first line of defense. Staying hydrated is also important. A way to tell whether you are hydrated is to view the color of the urine. If it is light yellow, you are probably hydrated. If it is darker, you might be dehydrated. If it is clear, you might be overhydrated.

The benefits of exercise have been shown to combat the side effects associated with menopause. Running in particular seems to play a major role in mitigating many of the effects of menopause. Many women who run during menopause say that running relieves these symptoms. Women who exercise say they experience fewer mood swings, less depression, and better short-term memory. Runners have greater bone density, which reduces the occurrence of bone fractures. And running reduces the chances of breast cancer and cardiovascular disease during menopause. Finally, it helps maintain libido.

During menopause, run how you feel. You don't have to push it or even stay on a strict schedule. Don't hesitate to run at a slower pace. This will help you deal with increased aches that might come with menopause. As always, running with a friend is beneficial. And, don't forget to include resistance exercises in your program. If you keep a running diary, you will see patterns develop that can help you make training decisions.

PART II

Program Planning

Challenge is necessary for improvement, but the challenges must not exceed the body's ability to handle them. This is a CBS approach: challenging but safe. Athletes thrive on challenge, but improvement comes from a balanced program that includes the right mix of the right components.

All worthwhile training programs—whether they are for fitness runners or serious competitors—address three basic questions: How long? How hard? How often? You must train long enough, hard enough, and often enough to stimulate the improvements you are seeking. Yet you must balance the work with recovery and take proper care of your body both on and off the track, trail, or road; otherwise, you risk exhaustion or injury, which could halt your progress. All training is a balancing act between *too little, just right,* and *too much.*

The answers to the three questions and correctly mixing training components vary, of course, according to each runner's ability and personal goals.

The approach to training outlined in this book is equally applicable to the elderly and the young, men and women, beginners and veterans. This section of the book explains the essential components of a successful program and guides you through the process of selecting and adjusting components to fit your particular needs.

7

Program Setup

At the heart of this chapter is the concept of $\dot{V}O_2max$, which, as noted in chapter 1, is shorthand for the volume of oxygen consumed at maximal effort (also known as *maximal oxygen uptake*). It is measured in milliliters per kilogram of body weight per minute (ml/kg/min). Because $\dot{V}O_2max$ is a vital indicator of endurance fitness, it underlies all the workouts and training schedules in this book.

An inactive but healthy adult might have a $\dot{V}O_2max$ of about 31 ml/kg/min, which would make it possible to run a mile in about 9 minutes. An excellent runner might have a $\dot{V}O_2max$ of about 75 ml/kg/min, which would make it possible to run a mile in about 4:10.

If both of these people weigh 154 pounds (70 kg), the inactive person would use 19,530 milliliters of oxygen during the mile run. The very fit runner would use 22,052 milliliters. We can look at these amounts in another way. A soft-drink can holds 355 milliliters. The inactive person used 55 cans of oxygen during the mile, and the skilled runner used 62 in less than half the time. How well you consume oxygen determines how fast you can run.

Your $\dot{V}O_2max$ is one of the most reliable ways to gauge your capacity for endurance activity. And it isn't a fixed figure; it changes with your fitness level. Therefore, you need to know your current level to determine the amount and pace of training you can handle right now. Then you can take the next steps to set up your training program.

Step 1: Find Your $\dot{V}O_2max$ Training Level

You can accurately estimate your $\dot{V}O_2max$ training level based on the distance you can cover in 12 minutes or from the result of a race run within the last month.

$\dot{V}O_2max$ Training Level From a 12-Minute Test

1. Select a trail, road, or track where you can measure distance or laps.
2. Start running at a pace you believe you can maintain for 12 minutes.
3. With about 2 minutes remaining, pick up the pace if you are able.

4. You should finish feeling tired and exhilarated, not exhausted.

5. Calculate the distance you covered in 12 minutes (for example, 6 laps of a 400-meter track, or 2.4 kilometers).

6. Refer to table 1.7 (see page 15) to look up the $\dot{V}O_2$max value closest to that distance (in our example 38). If the distance falls between two values, choose the lower one.

7. Use this number when you set up your training program.

$\dot{V}O_2$max Training Level From a Recent Race

1. Find the distance you raced within the past month (for example, 5K) on table 7.1.

Table 7.1 Correlating Race Results With $\dot{V}O_2$max

V.O₂max	Mile/1,500 m	5K	10K	Half marathon	Marathon
22	12:48/11:55	42:16	1:27:50	3:14:25	7:11:34
24	11:49/11:01	39:09	1:21:22	3:00:03	6:40:08
26	10:59/10:14	38:30	1:15:51	2:47:46	6:13:15
28	10:16/9:34	34:12	1:11:04	2:37:09	5:49:58
30	9:38/8:58	32:11	1:08:53	2:27:52	5:29:36
32	9:05/8:28	30:25	1:03:12	2:19:41	5:11:37
34	8:35/8:00	28:50	59:55	2:12:24	4:55:37
36	8:09/7:36	27:26	59:59	2:05:54	4:41:18
38	7:45/7:13	26:09	54:20	2:00:02	4:28:23
40	7:24/6:54	25:00	51:57	1:54:43	4:16:41
42	7:05/6:36	23:57	49:46	1:49:53	4:06:02
44	6:47/6:19	23:00	47:46	1:45:28	3:56:17
46	6:31/6:04	22:07	45:56	1:41:25	3:47:19
48	6:16/5:50	21:18	44:15	1:37:40	3:39:04
50	6:02/5:37	20:33	42:42	1:34:13	3:31:26
52	5:49/5:25	19:51	41:15	1:31:01	3:24:21
54	5:37/5:14	19:13	39:54	1:28:02	3:17:45
56	5:26/5:03	18:36	38:39	1:25:15	3:11:36
58	5:16/4:54	18:02	37:28	1:22:39	3:08:51
60	5:06/4:45	17:31	36:22	1:20:13	3:00:27
62	4:57/4:36	17:01	35:20	1:17:56	2:55:23
64	4:49/4:29	16:33	34:22	1:15:47	2:50:36
66	4:41/4:22	16:06	33:27	1:13:45	2:46:06
68	4:33/4:14	15:41	32:35	1:11:50	2:41:51
70	4:26/4:07	15:18	31:46	1:10:01	2:37:50

2. Select the finish time for that race (for example, 26:09).
3. Look up the $\dot{V}O_2$max volume closest to that time (in our example 38). If your time falls between two values, choose the lower one.
4. Set up your training program based on that $\dot{V}O_2$max value.

Step 2: Choose a Training Purpose

How you train depends on what you want to accomplish. Decide which of these levels most closely fits your interests and abilities:

- Train for health and fitness
- Train to race

If you would like to train for health and fitness, go to table 7.2 to choose a duration and then to step 6 to choose your training program. If you want to train to race, go to step 3, and choose a race goal.

Table 7.2 Determining Run Duration Based on Fraction of Maximum Run

Maximum run	25%	50%	67%
20 min	5 min	10 min	14 min
30 min	8 min	15 min	20 min
40 min	10 min	20 min	27 min
50 min	13 min	25 min	34 min
60 min	15 min	30 min	40 min
70 min	18 min	35 min	47 min
80 min	20 min	40 min	54 min
90 min	23 min	45 min	60 min
100 min	25 min	50 min	67 min
110 min	28 min	55 min	74 min
120 min	30 min	60 min	80 min

Step 3: Choose a Race Goal

How you train and for how long depends on your race distance.

1. Select the race distance for which you plan to train. Note the length of the training period for that distance.
   - **1 mile or 1,500 meters:** 13 weeks
   - **5K:** 13 weeks
   - **10K:** 15 weeks
   - **Half marathon:** 18 weeks
   - **Marathon:** 26 weeks

2. Count the number of weeks back from the race date and start your training program on the Sunday of that week.

3. Get your goal time from table 7.1 by selecting a $\dot{V}O_2max$ two numbers higher than your current level. For example, if your current $\dot{V}O_2max$ is 38 (5K in 26:09), your goal is the 5K time that correlates to a $\dot{V}O_2max$ of 40 (25:00).

4. Use the goal $\dot{V}O_2max$ for all training-related paces and intensities.

Step 4: Choose a Long-Run Duration

Longer-than-normal runs figure prominently in the training programs in this book. To find out where you should start, answer this question: If today were day 1 of your training program, what is longest you could run in a single training session and still be able to safely repeat the number of minutes on day 3? Choose from the following list.

20 minutes	80 minutes
30 minutes	90 minutes
40 minutes	100 minutes
50 minutes	110 minutes
60 minutes	120 minutes
70 minutes	

You determine the length of your shorter runs based on your current maximum run. Table 7.2 shows the number of minutes to run for different percentages of the long run.

Step 5: Find Your Running Intensity

Your efforts will vary widely, depending on the intent of the day's workout. The four effort levels used in this book are based on percentages of your $\dot{V}O_2$max:

1. **Easy:** 50 to 60 percent of $\dot{V}O_2$max
2. **Moderate:** 60 to 70 percent of $\dot{V}O_2$max
3. **Somewhat strong (SWS):** 75 to 85 percent of $\dot{V}O_2$max
4. **Strong:** 90 to 100 percent of $\dot{V}O_2$max

Intensities near or above 85 percent will take your body above the anaerobic threshold, and you will stimulate another energy system to help do the work. This energy system will increase the number of hydrogen ions produced and might cause discomfort.

Table 7.3 lists paces at the four effort levels. At some fitness levels, *easy* might mean walking, and *moderate* might mean mixing running with walking. *Strong* gives paces for distances less than a mile (1,600 m). Use the strong level of effort only for interval workouts and speed work and when you are preparing for a race.

Table 7.3   Finding Training Intensity

Easy range		
$\dot{V}O_2$max	50% $\dot{V}O_2$max	60% $\dot{V}O_2$max
22	25:36 mile/15:55 km	21:20 mile/13:12 km
24	23:38 mile/14:37 km	19:42 mile/12:13 km
26	21:58 mile/13:38 km	18:18 mile/11:20 km
28	20:31 mile/12:42 km	17:06 mile/10:36 km
30	19:16 mile/12:00 km	16:03 mile/9:55 km
32	18:10 mile/11:17 km	15:05 mile/9:22 km
34	17:11 mile/10:40 km	14:19 mile/8:52 km
36	16:18 mile/10:06 km	13:35 mile/8:26 km
38	15:31 mile/9:36 km	12:56 mile/8:00 km
40	14:48 mile/9:00 km	12:20 mile/7:37 km
42	14:09 mile/8:45 km	11:48 mile/7:19 km
44	13:34 mile/8:26 km	11:18 mile/7:00 km
46	13:01 mile/8:04 km	10:51 mile/6:42 km
48	12:32 mile/8:22 km	10:26 mile/6:27 km
50	12:04 mile/7:30 km	10:03 mile/6:12 km
52	11:38 mile/7:12 km	9:42 mile/6:01 km

> continued

Table 7.3   Finding Training Intensity > *continued*

Easy range *(continued)*

$\dot{V}O_2$max	50% $\dot{V}O_2$max	60% $\dot{V}O_2$max
54	11:15 mile/6:57 km	9:22 mile/5:50 km
56	10:53 mile/6:45 km	9:04 mile/5:39 km
58	10:32 mile/6:30 km	8:47 mile/5:28 km
60	10:13 mile/6:19 km	8:31 mile/5:16 km
62	9:54 mile/6:10 km	8:15 mile/5:05 km
64	9:37 mile/5:57 km	8:01 mile/4:58 km
66	9:21 mile/5:46 km	7:48 mile/4:50 km
68	9:06 mile/5:38 km	7:35 mile/4:42 km
70	8:52 mile/5:31 km	7:23 mile/4:35 km

Moderate range

$\dot{V}O_2$max	60% $\dot{V}O_2$max	70% $\dot{V}O_2$max
22	21:20 mile/13:12 km	18:17 mile/11:20 km
24	19:42 mile/12:09 km	16:53 mile/10:28 km
26	18:18 mile/11:20 km	15:41 mile/9:44 km
28	17:06 mile/10:36 km	14:40 mile/9:06 km
30	16:03 mile/9:55 km	13:46 mile/8:34 km
32	15:08 mile/9:22 km	12:58 mile/8:04 km
34	14:19 mile/8:52 km	12:16 mile/7:37 km
36	13:35 mile/8:26 km	11:39 mile/7:11 km
38	12:56 mile/8:00 km	11:05 mile/6:53 km
40	12:20 mile/7:38 km	10:34 mile/6:34 km
42	11:48 mile/7:19 km	10:07 mile/6:16 km
44	11:18 mile/7:00 km	9:41 mile/6:00 km
46	10:51 mile/6:42 km	9:18 mile/5:46 km
48	10:26 mile/6:27 km	8:57 mile/5:31 km
50	10:03 mile/6:12 km	8:37 mile/5:20 km
52	9:42 mile/6:01 km	8:19 mile/5:09 km
54	9:22 mile/5:50 km	8:02 mile/5:00 km
56	9:04 mile/5:38 km	7:46 mile/4:50 km
58	8:47 mile/5:28 km	7:31 mile/4:39 km
60	8:31 mile/5:16 km	7:18 mile/4:31 km
62	8:15 mile/5:05 km	7:05 mile/4:24 km
64	8:01 mile/4:58 km	6:52 mile/4:17 km
66	7:48 mile/4:50 km	6:41 mile/4:09 km
68	7:35 mile/4:42 km	6:30 mile/4:02 km
70	7:23 mile/4:35 km	6:20 mile/3:54 km

Somewhat strong range

$\dot{V}O_2$max	75% $\dot{V}O_2$max	85% $\dot{V}O_2$max
22	17:04 mile/10:36 km	15:45 mile/9:44 km
24	15:45 mile/9:46 km	13:54 mile/8:37 km
26	14:39 mile/9:03 km	12:55 mile/8:00 km
28	13:41 mile/8:30 km	12:04 mile/7:30 km
30	12:51 mile/7:45 km	11:20 mile/7:00 km
32	12:06 mile/7:30 km	10:41 mile/6:38 km
34	11:27 mile/7:04 km	10:06 mile/6:16 km
36	10:52 mile/6:45 km	9:35 mile/5:57 km
38	10:21 mile/6:23 km	9:08 mile/5:34 km
40	9:52 mile/6:08 km	8:42 mile/5:24 km
42	9:26 mile/5:50 km	8:20 mile/5:09 km
44	9:03 mile/5:36 km	7:59 mile/4:58 km
46	8:41 mile/5:24 km	7:40 mile/4:47 km
48	8:21 mile/5:11 km	7:22 mile/4:31 km
50	8:03 mile/4:58 km	7:06 mile/4:24 km
52	7:46 mile/4:50 km	6:51 mile/4:15 km
54	7:30 mile/4:39 km	6:37 mile/4:06 km
56	7:15 mile/4:30 km	6:24 mile/3:58 km
58	7:01 mile/4:20 km	6:12 mile/3:50 km
60	6:48 mile/4:13 km	6:00 mile/3:43 km
62	6:36 mile/4:06 km	5:50 mile/3:36 km
64	6:25 mile/3:58 km	5:40 mile/3:30 km
66	6:14 mile/3:50 km	5:30 mile/3:24 km
68	6:04 mile/3:45 km	5:21 mile/3:17 km
70	5:55 mile/3:39 km	5:13 mile/3:13 km

Strong range

$\dot{V}O_2$ max	90% $\dot{V}O_2$max	100% $\dot{V}O_2$max
22	14:13 mile/8:48 km	12:45/7:48
24	13:08 mile/8:07 km	11:45/7:15
26	12:12 mile/7:34 km	10:51/6:45
28	11:24 mile/7:04 km	10:15/6:15
30	10:42 mile/6:38 km	9:27/5:48
32	10:05 mile/6:15 km	9:06/5:36
34	9:33 mile/5:54 km	8:40/5:00
36	9:03 mile/5:36 km	8:09/4:51
38	8:37 mile/5:20 km	7:42/4:42
40	8:13 mile/5:05 km	7:40/4:33

> continued

Table 7.3   Finding Training Intensity > *continued*

Strong range *(continued)*

$\dot{V}O_2$ max	90% $\dot{V}O_2$max	100% $\dot{V}O_2$max
42	7:52 mile/4:54 km	6:54/4:03
44	7:32 mile/4:39 km	6:42/3:57
46	7:14 mile/4:28 km	6:21/3:51
48	6:58 mile/4:20 km	6:00/3:45
50	6:42 mile/4:09 km	5:51/3:39
52	6:26 mile/3:58 km	5:42/3:24
54	6:15 mile/3:51 km	5:36/3:18
56	6:03 mile/3:45 km	5:18/3:15
58	5:51 mile/3:37 km	5:00/3:00
60	5:40 mile/3:32 km	4:54/2:54
62	5:30 mile/3:25 km	4:48/2:51
64	5:21 mile/3:19 km	4:42/2:48
66	5:12 mile/3:13 km	4:39/2:45
68	5:03 mile/3:06 km	4:33/2:42
70	4:56 mile/3:02 km	4:18/2:39

Strong range for intervals or speed

$\dot{V}O_2$max	%	100 m	150 m	200 m	300 m	400 m	800 m
22	90	:51	1:27	1:43	2:35	3:28	7:00
	110	:42	1:03	1:24	2:07	2:50	5:44
24	90	:47	1:21	1:35	2:23	3:12	6:28
	110	:38	1:00	1:28	1:57	2:37	5:17
26	90	:44	1:06	1:28	2:13	2:58	6:01
	110	:36	:52	1:12	1:49	2:26	4:55
28	90	:41	1:01	1:22	2:04	2:47	5:37
	110	:33	:50	1:07	1:42	2:16	4:36
30	90	:38	:58	1:17	1:57	2:37	5:16
	110	:31	:47	1:03	1:36	2:08	4:19
32	90	:36	:54	1:13	1:50	2:28	4:58
	110	:30	:45	1:00	1:30	2:01	4:04
34	90	:34	:51	1:09	1:44	2:20	4:42
	110	:28	:42	:56	1:25	1:54	3:51
36	90	:32	:49	1:06	1:39	2:12	4:28
	110	:27	:40	:54	1:21	1:48	3:39
38	90	:31	:47	1:02	1:34	2:06	4:15
	110	:25	:38	:51	1:17	1:43	3:38
40	90	:29	:44	:59	1:30	2:00	4:03
	110	:24	:36	:49	1:13	1:38	3:19

$\dot{V}O_2$max	%	100 m	150 m	200 m	300 m	400 m	800 m
Strong range for intervals or speed *(continued)*								
42	90	:28	:42	:57	1:26	1:55	3:52
	110	:23	:35	:47	1:10	1:34	3:10
44	90	:27	:41	:55	1:22	1:50	3:43
	110	:22	:34	:45	1:07	1:30	3:02
46	90	:26	:39	:52	1:19	1:46	3:34
	110	:21	:32	:43	1:05	1:27	2:55
48	90	:25	:37	:50	1:16	1:42	3:26
	110	:20	:30	:41	1:02	1:23	2:48
50	90	:24	:36	:48	1:13	1:38	3:18
	110	:20	:30	:40	1:00	1:20	2:42
52	90	:23	:35	:47	1:11	1:35	3:11
	110	:19	:28	:38	:58	1:17	2:36
54	90	:22	:34	:45	1:08	1:31	3:05
	110	:18	:27	:37	:56	1:15	2:31
56	90	:22	:33	:44	1:06	1:28	2:59
	110	:18	:27	:36	:54	1:12	2:26
58	90	:21	:30	:42	1:04	1:26	2:53
	110	:17	:26	:35	:52	1:10	2:21
60	90	:20	:30	:41	1:02	1:23	2:48
	110	:17	:25	:34	:51	1:08	2:17
62	90	:20	:30	:40	1:00	1:21	2:43
	110	:16	:24	:33	:49	1:06	2:13
64	90	:19	:28	:39	:58	1:18	2:38
	110	:16	:23	:32	:48	1:04	2:09
66	90	:19	:28	:38	:57	1:16	2:34
	110	:15	:22	:31	:46	1:02	2:06
68	90	:18	:27	:37	:55	1:14	2:29
	110	:15	:22	:30	:45	1:01	2:02
70	90	:18	:27	:36	:54	1:12	2:26
	110	:14	:21	:29	:44	:59	1:59

Step 6: Construct Your Training Plan

Do you feel overwhelmed by numbers? You've been asked to do considerable calculating, but it's necessary and valuable for individualizing your training. The numbers represent the framework on which you can build your personal training program.

Use figure 7.1 to construct this framework. Once you have this information, you will be able to easily record your weekly training in your diary.

Figure 7.1 Your Training Program

Following the instructions in this chapter, fill in the answers that apply to your current running and immediate goals. Use this information to build your training program.

1. What is your $\dot{V}O_2$max?

    From a 12-minute run–walk test:

    Distance covered _____

    $\dot{V}O_2$max _____

    From a recent race result:

    Distance _____

    Time _____

    $\dot{V}O_2$max _____

2. What is your training purpose?

    Training for fitness _____

    Training to race _____

3. What is your race goal? (If you don't plan to race, skip to question 4.)

    Race distance _____

    Length of training program _____

    Race date _____

    Date training starts _____

    Goal time for the race _____

    Goal pace (per mile or km) _____

4. What is your long-run duration?

    Current maximum time _____

    Two-thirds of maximum time _____

    One-half of maximum time _____

    One-fourth of maximum time _____

5. What is your training intensity (pace per mile or km)?

    Easy range 50% _____ 60% _____

    Moderate range 60% _____ 70% _____

    Somewhat strong range 75% _____ 85% _____

    Strong range (mile, or 1,600 km) 90% _____ 100% _____

    Strong range (100-800 meters)

        100 m 90% _____ 110% _____

        150 m 90% _____ 110% _____

        200 m 90% _____ 110% _____

        300 m 90% _____ 110% _____

        400 m 90% _____ 110% _____

        800 m 90% _____ 110% _____

8

Types of Running Workouts

In cooking you achieve satisfying results by combining high-quality ingredients using proven recipes to create a tasty, nutritious meal. The same is true when combining workouts in a training program. Therefore, this book takes a cookbook approach to developing a training program, although it offers more flexibility in combining ingredients than most cookbooks do.

First, you'll have a chance to become familiar with the primary ingredients by reading the detailed descriptions of types of workouts. In the remaining chapters in part II you learn about the other ingredients—those that add flavor and essential nutrients to ensure that your "training diet" is well balanced. In part III you will find the recipes for combining the ingredients to create a successful running program.

This book outlines just eight types of workout. However, within each type, the sessions are extremely flexible so you can vary the length and pace to fit your ability and goal. The types of workouts you will build your training program from are listed in table 8.1. Descriptions and instructions for the workout options are described in the text following the tables (tables 8.2-8.4), moving from the slowest and easiest sessions to the fastest and hardest. When in doubt in training and racing, be conservative, except in the last half of your goal race. Then, if in doubt, be intelligently aggressive.

Note that workouts are given priority numbers throughout part III. The most important session of the week is priority 1, the least important is priority 7. If you are planning to train four days a week, you should schedule priorities 1, 2, 3, and 4.

Table 8.1 Types of Workouts

SWS means somewhat strong. You can substitute workouts as noted: fartlek for steady state, out and back for tempo, and new interval for interval.

Workout	Pace or intensity	% $\dot{V}O_2$max	Time or distance
Recovery	Easy	50-60	1/4 to 1/2 max time
Long	Moderate	60-70	Max time
Steady state or fartlek	SWS	75-85	2/3 max time
Tempo or out and back	SWS to strong	85-95	1/2 max time
Interval or new interval	Strong	90-110	200 m, 300 m, 400 m
Speed	Strong	90-110	100 m, 150 m
Race prep	Goal pace	100	800 m, 1,500 m, 1 mile, 2 miles
Race	Goal pace	100	Mile to marathon

Table 8.2 Metric and English Conversions

Metric distances	English equivalents
50 m	54.68 yd
100 m	109.36 yd
150 m	164.04 yd
200 m	218.72 yd
300 m	328.08 yd
400 m	437.44 yd
500 m	526.81 yd
600 m	656.17 yd
800 m	874.88 yd
1,000 m	1,093.61 yd
1,200 m	1,312.33 yd
1,500 m	.93 mile (1,620.42 yd)
1,600 m	.99 mile
3,000 m	.86 mile
3,200 m	1.98 miles
5,000 m	3.11 miles
8,000 m	4.97 miles
10,000 m	6.21 miles
12K	7.46 miles
15K	9.32 miles
20K	12.43 miles
Half marathon (21.1K)	13.11 miles
25K	15.54 miles
30K	18.64 miles
Marathon (42.2K)	26.22 miles

English distances	Metric equivalents
50 yd	45.72 m
100 yd	91.44 m
110 yd	100.58 m
150 yd	137.16 m
220 yd (1/8 mile)	201.67 m
330 yd	301.64 m
440 yd (1/4 mile)	402.34 m
550 yd	502.92 m
660 yd (3/8 mile)	603.50 m
880 yd (1/2 mile)	804.67 m
1,100 yd (5/8 mile)	1,006.34 m
1,320 yd (3/4 mile)	1,207.01 m
1 mile	1,609 m
2 miles	3,218 m
5 miles	8.01 km
10 miles	16.09 km
Half marathon (13.1 miles)	21.10 km
20 miles	32.18 km
Marathon (26.2 miles)	42.19 km

Table 8.3   Finding per Mile and per Kilometer Pace

Mile/ kilometer	1,500 m	5K	10K	Half marathon	Marathon
4:00/2:28	3:43				
4:10/2:35	3:53	12:56			
4:20/2:42	4:02	13:27	26:54		
4:30/2:48	4:11	13:58	27:56		
4:40/2:54	4:21	14:29	28:58	1:01:11	
4:50/3:00	4:30	15:00	30:00	1:03:22	2:06:44
5:00/3:06	4:40	15:30	31:00	1:05:33	2:11:06
5:10/3:13	4:49	16:01	32:02	1:07:44	2:15:28
5:20/3:19	4:58	16:32	33:04	1:09:55	2:19:50
5:30/3:25	5:07	17:03	34:06	1:12:06	2:24:12
5:40/3:31	5:17	17:34	35:08	1:14:17	2:28:34
5:50/3:38	5:26	18:05	36:10	1:16:28	2:32:56
6:00/3:44	5:36	18:36	37:12	1:18:40	2:37:19
6:10/3:50	5:45	19:07	38:14	1:20:51	2:41:41
6:20/3:56	5:54	19:38	39:16	1:23:02	2:46:03
6:30/4:02	6:03	20:09	40:18	1:25:13	2:50:12

> continued

Table 8.3   Finding per Mile and per Kilometer Pace > *continued*

Mile/ kilometer	1,500 m	5K	10K	Half marathon	Marathon
6:40/4:09	6:12	20:40	41:20	1:27:24	2:54:47
6:50/4:15	6:21	21:11	42:22	1:29:35	2:59:09
7:00/4:21	6:31	21:42	43:24	1:31:47	3:03:33
7:10/4:27	6:40	22:13	44:26	1:33:28	3:07:55
7:20/4:33	6:49	22:44	45:28	1:36:09	3:12:17
7:30/4:40	6:59	23:15	46:30	1:38:20	3:16:39
7:40/4:46	7:08	23:46	47:32	1:40:31	3:21:01
7:50/4:52	7:16	24:17	48:34	1:42:42	3:25:23
8:00/4:58	7:27	24:48	49:36	1:44:53	3:29:45
8:10/5:05	7:36	25:19	50:38	1:47:04	3:34:07
8:20/5:11	7:45	25:50	51:40	1:49:15	3:38:29
8:30/5:17	7:55	26:21	52:42	1:51:26	3:42:51
8:40/5:23	8:04	26:52	53:44	1:53:37	3:47:13
8:50/5:29	8:14	27:23	54:46	1:55:43	3:51:35
9:00/5:36	8:23	27:54	55:48	1:58:00	3:56:00
9:10/5:42	8:33	28:25	56:50	2:00:11	4:00:22
9:20/5:48	8:42	28:56	57:52	2:02:22	4:04:44
9:30/5:54	8:52	29:27	58:54	2:04:33	4:09:06
9:40/6:00	9:01	29:58	59:56	2:06:44	4:09:06
9:50/6:06	9:11	30:29	1:00:58	2:08:55	4:17:50
10:00/6:12	9:20	31:00	1:02:00	2:11:00	4:22:00
10:10/6:18	9:29	31:31	1:03:02	2:13:11	4:26:22
10:20/6:24	9:38	32:02	1:04:04	2:15:22	4:30:44
10:30/6:30	9:47	32:33	1:05:06	2:17:33	4:35:06
10:40/6:36	9:56	33:04	1:06:08	2:19:44	4:39:28
10:50/6:42	10:06	33:35	1:07:10	2:21:55	4:44:50
11:00/6:49	10:15	34:06	1:08:12	2:24:06	4:48:12
11:10/6:55	10:24	34:37	1:09:14	2:26:18	4:52:36
11:20/7:01	10:33	35:08	1:10:16	2:28:29	4:56:58
11:30/7:07	10:43	35:39	1:11:18	2:30:40	5:01:20
11:40/7:13	10:52	36:10	1:12:20	2:32:21	5:04:42
11:50/7:20	11:02	36:41	1:13:22	2:34:32	5:09:04
12:00/7:27	11:11	37:12	1:14:24	2:36:44	5:13:26
12:10/7:33	11:20	37:43	1:15:26	2:38:55	5:17:48
12:20/7:39	11:30	38:14	1:16:28	2:41:06	5:22:10
12:30/7:45	11:39	38:45	1:17:30	2:43:17	5:26:32
12:40/7:51	11:48	39:16	1:18:32	2:45:28	5:30:54

Mile/kilometer	1,500 m	5K	10K	Half marathon	Marathon
12:50/7:57	11:58	39:47	1:19:34	2:47:39	5:35:18
13:00/8:04	12:07	40:18	1:20:36	2:49:50	5:39:40
13:10/8:10	12:16	40:49	1:21:38	2:52:01	5:44:02
13:20/8:16	12:26	41:20	1:22:40	2:54:12	5:48:24
13:30/8:22	12:35	41:51	1:23:42	2:56:23	5:52:46
13:40/8:28	12:44	42:22	1:24:44	2:58:34	5:57:08
13:50/8:34	12:54	42:53	1:25:46	3:00:45	6:01:30
14:00/8:41	13:03	43:24	1:26:48	3:02:56	6:05:52
14:10/8:47	13:12	43:55	1:27:50	3:05:07	6:10:14
14:20/8:53	13:22	44:26	1:28:52	3:07:18	6:14:36
14:30/8:59	12:31	44:57	1:29:54	3:09:29	6:18:58
14:40/9:05	12:40	45:28	1:30:56	3:11:40	6:23:20
14:50/9:11	12:50	45:59	1:31:58	3:13:51	6:27:42

Table 8.4 Training Paces (100-800 m)

Mile/kilometer	100 m	150 m	200 m	300 m	400 m	800 m
4:00/2:28	:15	:23	:30	:45	1:00	2:00
4:10/2:35	:15	:24	:31	:46	1:02	2:05
4:20/2:42	:16	:25	:32	:48	1:05	2:10
4:30/2:48	:16	:26	:33	:50	1:07	2:15
4:40/2:54	:17	:27	:35	:52	1:10	2:20
4:50/3:00	:18	:27	:36	:54	1:12	2:25
5:00/3:06	:18	:28	:37	:56	1:15	2:30
5:10/3:13	:19	:29	:38	:58	1:17	2:35
5:20/3:19	:20	:30	:40	1:00	1:20	2:40
5:30/3:25	:20	:31	:41	1:01	1:22	2:45
5:40/3:31	:21	:32	:42	1:03	1:25	2:50
5:50/3:38	:21	:33	:43	1:05	1:27	2:55
6:00/3:44	:22	:34	:45	1:07	1:30	3:00
6:10/3:50	:23	:35	:46	1:09	1:32	3:05
6:20/3:56	:23	:36	:47	1:10	1:35	3:10
6:30/4:02	:24	:37	:48	1:12	1:37	3:15
6:40/4:09	:25	:38	:50	1:15	1:40	3:20
6:50/4:15	:26	:38	:51	1:17	1:42	3:25
7:00/4:21	:26	:39	:52	1:19	1:45	3:30
7:10/4:27	:26	:40	:53	1:20	1:47	3:35

> continued

Table 8.4   Training Paces (100-800 m) > *continued*

Mile/kilometer	100 m	150 m	200 m	300 m	400 m	800 m
7:20/4:33	:27	:41	:55	1:22	1:50	3:40
7:30/4:40	:28	:42	:56	1:24	1:52	3:45
7:40/4:46	:28	:43	:57	1:26	1:55	3:50
7:50/4:52	:29	:44	:58	1:28	1:57	3:55
8:00/4:58	:30	:45	1:00	1:30	2:00	4:00
8:10/5:05	:30	:46	1:01	1:31	2:03	4:05
8:20/5:11	:31	:47	1:02	1:33	2:06	4:10
8:30/5:17	:31	:48	1:03	1:35	2:07	4:15
8:40/5:23	:32	:49	1:05	1:37	2:10	4:20
8:50/5:29	:33	:49	1:06	1:39	2:12	4:25
9:00/5:36	:33	:50	1:07	1:41	2:15	4:30
9:10/5:42	:34	:51	1:08	1:43	2:17	4:35
9:20/5:48	:35	:52	1:10	1:45	2:20	4:40
9:30/5:54	:35	:53	1:11	1:47	2:22	4:45
9:40/6:00	:36	:54	1:12	1:48	2:25	4:50
9:50/6:06	:36	:55	1:13	1:50	2:27	4:55
10:00/6:12	:37	:56	1:15	1:53	2:30	5:00
10:10/6:18	:38	:57	1:16	1:55	2:32	5:05
10:20/6:24	:39	:58	1:18	1:57	2:35	5:10
10:30/6:30	:39	:59	1:19	1:58	2:37	5:15
10:40/6:36	:40	1:00	1:20	2:00	2:40	5:20
10:50/6:42	:40	1:01	1:21	2:02	2:42	5:25
11:00/6:49	:41	1:02	1:23	2:04	2:45	5:30
11:10/6:55	:42	1:03	1:24	2:06	2:47	5:35
11:20/7:01	:42	1:04	1:25	2:07	2:50	5:40
11:30/7:07	:43	1:05	1:26	2:09	2:52	5:45
11:40/7:13	:44	1:06	1:28	2:12	2:55	5:50
11:50/7:20	:45	1:07	1:29	2:14	2:57	5:55

Description: These are the easiest training days of the week, other than rest days. But that doesn't mean they're unimportant. Recovery days, like rest, help the body prepare for harder days. The pace is easy and the distances are relatively short on recovery days. You can mix running and walking, or even mix brief runs into what is mostly a walk.

Priority: Low, with a rating of 5, 6, or 7 (priority 1 being the most important, 7 the least). These runs are the first to be replaced by rest or cross-training days.

Duration: One-fourth to one-half of current maximum running time or distance

Pace or effort: Easy

Percentage of $\dot{V}O_2$max: 50 to 60 percent. See table 7.3 to calculate your pace based on $\dot{V}O_2$max.

Warm-up: Nothing formal, except possibly a 5-minute walk before starting to run. Otherwise treat the first 5 to 10 minutes as a warm-up by running at slower-than-normal pace.

Cool-down: Possibly a 5-minute walk and then stretching exercises.

Typical workouts: For a fitness runner with a 36 $\dot{V}O_2$max and a max run time of 30 minutes: 15 minutes at 13:35 to 16:18 per mile (8:26-10:06/km).

For a mile to 10K runner with a 50 $\dot{V}O_2$max and max run time of 60 minutes: 30 minutes at 10:03 to 12:04 per mile (6:12-7:30/km).

For a half marathon to marathon runner with a 50 $\dot{V}O_2$max and a max run time of 90 minutes: 45 minutes at 10:03 to 12:04 per mile (6:15-7:30/km).

LONG RUNS

Description: *Long* is in the eye of the beholder, meaning this type of workout is at least one-third longer than what you normally run. These runs begin to build an endurance base in fitness runners and firm up that base in competitive runners. For the fitness runner it also makes the standard runs seem a little shorter. For half marathoners and marathoners it is a rehearsal of what they'll run on race day. For fitness runners walk breaks are an acceptable option during long runs.

Priority: High, always a rating of 1 (on a scale of 1 to 7) unless the week includes a second long run, which rates a 2.

Duration: Current maximum time or distance, plus additional minutes as assigned in each program's weekly schedule. Runs do not exceed 120 minutes, except in rare cases for marathoners.

Pace or effort: Moderate

Percentage of $\dot{V}O_2$max: 60 to 70 percent. See table 7.3 to calculate your pace based on $\dot{V}O_2$max. As the run progresses and you feel good, you can pick up the pace during the last half of the distance.

Warm-up: Nothing formal, except possibly a 5-minute walk before starting to run. Otherwise treat the first 5 to 10 minutes as a warm-up by running at slower-than-normal pace.

Cool-down: Possibly a 5-minute walk and then stretching exercises.

Typical workouts: For a fitness runner with a 36 $\dot{V}O_2$max and a max run time of 30 minutes: 30 minutes at 11:39 to 13:35 per mile (7:11-8:26/km).

For a mile to 10K runner with a 50 $\dot{V}O_2$max and max run time of 60 minutes: 60 minutes at 8:37 to 10:03 per mile (5:20-6:12/km).

For a half marathon to marathon runner with a 50 $\dot{V}O_2$max and a max run time of 90 minutes: 90 minutes at 8:37 to 10:03 per mile (5:20-6:12/km).

Description: Now the pace picks up as you transition between the slower-paced workouts that preceded this one and the higher-speed training that follows. You push the pace noticeably more than on recovery runs but cover about one-third less distance than in the long runs. This is the workout where you learn to run your most efficient training pace, which gives the most return for your effort.

Priority: High to medium, with a rating of 1, 2, or 3 (on a scale of 1 to 7), depending on the week and program. Note that many weeks include two or even three steady-state runs.

Duration: Two-thirds of your current maximum time or distance, plus additional minutes as assigned in each program's weekly schedule. Added time ranges from 1 to 10 minutes.

Pace or effort: Somewhat strong

Percentage of $\dot{V}O_2$max: 75 to 85 percent. See table 7.3 to calculate your pace based on $\dot{V}O_2$max.

Warm-up: Run easily or walk for 5 to 10 minutes.

Cool-down: Run easily or walk for 5 to 10 minutes and then stretch.

Typical workouts: For a fitness runner with a 36 $\dot{V}O_2$max and a max run time of 30 minutes: 20 minutes at 9:35 to 10:52 per mile (5:57-6:45/km).

For a mile to 10K runner with a 50 $\dot{V}O_2$max and max run time of 60 minutes: 40 minutes at 7:06 to 8:03 per mile (4:24-4:58/km).

For a half marathon to marathon runner with a 50 $\dot{V}O_2$max and a max run time of 90 minutes: 60 minutes at 7:06 to 8:03 per mile (4:24-4:58/km).

FARTLEK RUNS

Description: Fartlek means *speed play* in Swedish. You can substitute this workout for a steady-state run anytime. Here you simply play with speed. Part of the run is at an easy to moderate pace and part is at a pace you might run for a mile, 800 meters, or 400 meters. Play is the key word. Don't think you have to run moderately for 2 minutes and hard for 30 seconds. Have fun with the variety and keep changing it up. For example, during the course of the workout you could end up running three-quarters of it easy to moderate and one-quarter at faster speeds.

Priority: High to medium, with a rating of 1, 2, or 3 (on a scale of 1 to 7), depending on the week and program. Note that many weeks include two or even three fartlek runs.

Duration: Two-thirds of current maximum time or distance, plus additional minutes as assigned in each program's weekly schedule. Added time ranges from 1 to 10 minutes.

Pace or effort: Overall somewhat strong

Percentage of $\dot{V}O_2$max: Overall 75 to 85 percent. See table 7.3 to calculate your pace based on $\dot{V}O_2$max. The easy to moderate part might be a little slower and the speed part a little faster.

Warm-up: Run easily or walk for 5 to 10 minutes.

Cool-down: Run easily or walk for 5 to 10 minutes and then stretch.

Typical workouts: For a fitness runner with a 36 $\dot{V}O_2$max and a max run time of 30 minutes: Maybe 15 minutes easy to moderate and 5 minutes at various faster speeds.

For a mile to 10K runner with a 50 $\dot{V}O_2$max and max run time of 60 minutes: Maybe 30 minutes easy to moderate and 10 minutes at various faster speeds.

For a half marathon to marathon runner with a 50 $\dot{V}O_2$max and a max run time of 90 minutes: Maybe 45 minutes easy to moderate and 15 minutes at various faster speeds.

Description: *Tempo* is another word for *pace*. All runs have tempo, you might say, but here the word takes on a special meaning. In tempo runs you travel at close to your race pace but for a distance shorter than your goal race. A thorough warm-up is essential for this workout, and its faster pace helps your body adapt to the demands of racing.

Priority: High, with a rating of 1 or 2 (on a scale of 1 to 7). Note that tempo runs usually replace long runs.

Duration: One-half of current maximum time or distance. The actual length is shorter for track racers than for marathoners.

Pace or effort: Somewhat strong to strong

Percentage of $\dot{V}O_2$max: 85 to 95 percent. See table 7.3 to calculate your pace based on $\dot{V}O_2$max.

Warm-up: Run easily or run and walk for 5 to 10 minutes, then run 4 × 50-meter strides (at about the pace of the day's tempo run, with 50-meter recovery jog or walk) and then perform dynamic stretching exercises.

Cool-down: Repeat warm-up but without the strides. Then finish with static stretching.

Typical workouts: For a fitness runner with a 36 $\dot{V}O_2$max and a max run time of 30 minutes: 15 minutes at 8:15 to 9:35 per mile (5:07-5:57/km).

For a mile to 10 K runner with a 50 $\dot{V}O_2$max and max run time of 60 minutes: 40 minutes at 6:05 to 7:06 per mile (3:47-4:24/km).

For a half marathon to marathon runner with a 50 $\dot{V}O_2$max and a max run time of 90 minutes: 60 minutes at 6:05 to 7:06 per mile (3:47-4:24/km).

OUT-AND-BACK RUNS

Description: An *out-and-back* run can substitute for a tempo run anytime. These runs can be very enjoyable because you finish at a fast pace but feel very much in control. Divide the run in two equal time halves. During the first half, run at a pace you know you could handle for the entire time. At the halfway point, turn around and pick up the pace slightly for half the time remaining. Then pick it up again for half the time remaining. Do this until you are back where you started. The second half of the run will take less time than the first half.

Priority: High, with a rating of 1 or 2 (on a scale of 1 to 7). Note that out and backs can also replace long runs for those weeks.

Duration: One-half of current maximum time or distance. The actual length is shorter for track racers than for marathoners.

Pace or effort: Somewhat strong to strong

Percentage of $\dot{V}O_2$max: 85 to 95 percent. See table 7.3 to calculate your pace based on $\dot{V}O_2$max.

Warm-up: Run easily or run and walk for 5 to 10 minutes, then run 4 × 50-meter strides (at about the pace of the day's out and back run, with 50-meter recovery jog or walk), and then perform dynamic stretching exercises.

Cool-down: Repeat warm-up but without the strides. Then finish with static stretching.

Typical workouts: For a fitness runner with a 36 $\dot{V}O_2$max and a max run time of 30 minutes: Go out for 7:30 minutes at a pace between 8:15 and 9:35 per mile (5:07-5:57/km). Turn around and pick up the pace a little for the next 3:45. Pick it up again for the next 1:52. Pick it up again for the next 0:56. Pick it up again for 0:28 or until you reach your starting point.

For a mile or 10K runner with a 50 $\dot{V}O_2$max and max run time of 60 minutes: Go out for 20 minutes at a pace between 6:05 and 7:06 per mile (3:47-4:24/km). Turn around and pick up the pace a little for the next 10 minutes. Pick it up again for the next 5 minutes. Pick it up again for the next 2:30. Pick it up again for 1:15 or until you reach your starting point.

Description: Repetition training alternates fast and slow segments. Intervals are your most structured workouts, usually on a track and for specified distances with recovery periods of the same length between reps. They are run at race pace or slightly faster. The intensity prepares you for a strong finish in a race.

Priority: High to medium, with a rating of 1, 2, 3, or 4 (on a scale of 1 to 7), depending on the week and program. Note that most interval workouts are 2s and 3s.

Duration: 200, 300, or 400 meters (220, 330, 440 yds). The number of repeats depends on the length of the rep and the week and program. Recovery jogs and walks are equal to the length of the intervals.

Pace or effort: Strong

Percentage of $\dot{V}O_2max$: 90 to 110 percent. See table 7.3 to calculate your pace based on $\dot{V}O_2max$.

Warm-up: Run easily or run and walk for 5 to 10 minutes, perform dynamic stretching exercises, and then run 6 × 50-meter strides (at about the pace of the day's interval runs, with 50-meter recovery jogs or walks).

Cool-down: Repeat the warm-up but without the strides. Finish with static stretching.

Typical workouts: No interval workouts are scheduled for a fitness runner.

For a mile runner with a 50 $\dot{V}O_2max$: 5 × 300 meters in 1:00 to 1:13 each.

For a 5K to 10K runner with a 50 $\dot{V}O_2max$: 10 × 400 meters in 1:20 to 1:38 each.

For a half marathon to marathon runner with a 50 $\dot{V}O_2max$: 12 × 400 meters in 1:20 to 1:38 each.

NEW INTERVAL RUNS

Description: Coach Peter Thompson, chairman for IAAF long-distance running for 20 years and coach of numerous world-class and national runners, has developed an improvement to interval training, which he calls new interval training. This type of workout can be substituted for an interval run anytime. You can learn more about it at newintervaltraining.com. To turn a standard interval workout into a new interval session, you change the recovery between repetitions. Instead of jogging or walking during the recovery, you do a roll-on recovery in which you slow the pace but keep running. As you approach the next fast section, you increase the pace. The roll-on pace is up to you and will get faster with practice.

Priority: High to medium, with a rating of 1, 2, 3, or 4 (on a scale of 1 to 7), depending on the week and program. Note that most interval workouts are 2s and 3s.

Duration: 200, 300, or 400 meters (110, 220, 330, or 440 yds). The number of repeats varies by the length of the reps and the week and the program. Roll-on recovery between intervals should start at a length equal to the repetition.

Pace or effort: Strong

Percentage of $\dot{V}O_2$max: 90 to 100 percent. See table 7.3 to calculate your pace based on $\dot{V}O_2$max.

Warm-up: Run easily or run and walk for 5 to 10 minutes, perform dynamic stretching exercises, and then run 6 × 50-meter strides (at about the pace of the day's interval runs, with 50-meter recovery jogs or walks).

Cool-down: Repeat warm-up but without the strides. Finish with static stretching.

Typical workouts: No new interval workouts are scheduled for a fitness runner.

For a mile runner with a 50 $\dot{V}O_2$max: 5 × 300 meters in 1:00 to 1:13 each followed by a roll-on recovery.

For a 5K to 10K runner with a 50 $\dot{V}O_2$max: 10 × 400 meters in 1:20 to 1:38 each followed by a roll-on recovery.

For a half marathon to marathon runner with a 50 $\dot{V}O_2$max: 12 × 400 meters in 1:20 to 1:38 each followed by a roll-on recovery.

Description: Note that you're allowed here, even encouraged, to run fast. Speed runs don't last longer than 150 meters. They teach acceleration and faster leg turnover, which are especially valuable at the end of a race, and also make the overall race pace seem a little slower.

Priority: Medium, with a rating of 3 or 4 (on a scale of 1, highest, to 7, lowest).

Duration: 100 or 150 meters (110 or 165 yds). The number of repeats varies by the length of the reps and the week and the program. Recovery jogs or walks are equal to the length of the speed runs.

Pace or effort: Strong

Percentage of $\dot{V}O_2$max: 90 to 110 percent. See table 7.3 to calculate your pace based on $\dot{V}O_2$max.

Warm-up: Run easily or run and walk for 5 to 10 minutes, perform dynamic stretching exercises, then run 6 × 50-meter strides (at about the pace of the day's speed run, with 50-meter recovery jogs or walks), and then do dynamic stretching exercises.

Cool-down: Repeat the warm-up but without the strides and finish with static stretching.

Typical workouts: No speed workouts are scheduled for a fitness runner.

For milers to marathoners with a 50 $\dot{V}O_2$max: 12 × 100 meters in 20 to 24 seconds each.

Description: This workout consists of repetitions that are longer than those in other workout types. And you run them at your goal race pace, defined in this book as a $\dot{V}O_2$max level two points higher than your level when you began your program. Race-prep runs simulate racing better than any of the other workout types.

Priority: High to medium, with a rating of 1, 2, or 3 (on a scale of 1 to 7), depending on the week and program. Note that some weeks include two race preps.

Duration: 800 meters (880 yds), 1 mile and 2 miles (1,600 and 3,200 meters). The number of repeats varies according to the length of the rep and the week and the program. The length of recovery jogs and walks is equal to the length of the race-prep runs.

Pace or effort: Goal race pace (2 points higher than $\dot{V}O_2$max at beginning of program).

Percentage of $\dot{V}O_2$max: 100 percent. See table 7.3 to calculate your pace based on $\dot{V}O_2$max.

Warm-up: Run easily or run and walk for 5 to 10 minutes, perform dynamic stretching exercises, then run 6 × 50-meter strides (at about the pace of the day's race-prep runs, with 50-meter recovery jogs or walks).

Cool-down: Repeat the warm-up but without the strides, and finish with static stretching.

Typical workouts: No race-preparation workouts are scheduled for a fitness runner.

For a mile to 10K runner with a beginning $\dot{V}O_2$max of 50 and a goal-pace $\dot{V}O_2$max of 52: 5 × 800 meters in 2:31 to 3:05 each.

For a half marathon or marathon runner with a beginning $\dot{V}O_2$max of 50 and a goal-pace $\dot{V}O_2$max of 52: 5 × mile in 6:37 to 7:30 each.

Description: This is what you've been aiming for all along: the *big day*. Your training will have told you by now whether you're ready to reach your goal pace or not. I hope you are. Races less important than the target event might also be part of your buildup and replace some of the week's tempo runs.

Priority: Highest, a definite rating of 1, not only for that week but for the entire program. Note that all training tapers off for at least a week before the target race.

Duration: Distance for which you've trained from 1,500 meters to a marathon.

Pace or effort: Goal pace, two points higher than your $\dot{V}O_2max$ at the beginning of the program.

Percentage of $\dot{V}O_2max$: 100 percent

Warm-up: Run easily or run and walk for 5 to 10 minutes, perform dynamic stretching exercises, and then run 4×100-meter strides (at about the pace of the day's race, with 50-meter recovery jogs or walks). You might do more intervals for a shorter race and fewer for a longer distance.

Cool-down: Repeat the warm-up but without the strides, and then finish with static stretching.

The race: Start at or a little slower than your goal pace and try to slowly pick up the pace in the second half of the race (just like an out-and-back run). Don't make the mistake of going out too fast. It *rarely* works.

No races are scheduled for a health and fitness runner. However, you should try a low-key organized mile or 5K. It could be fun.

For a mile to 10K runner and a half marathon to marathon runner: Run your target race on the final week of the program.

9

Pre- and Postworkout Routines

Of course, the repetitions and sustained runs you do during your workouts are crucial for meeting your running goals. But they are not the only ingredients in a well-designed training program. A proper warm-up and cool-down will ensure you get the most from each workout and are ready for the next day's training. This chapter addresses these important components and also discusses meeting nutritional requirements before and after a workout.

Warm-Up and Cool-Down

What image comes to mind when you think of warm-up? It could be runners bending and stretching or perhaps leaning against walls or trees. These exercises have become standard in running training and for good reasons. When they are performed regularly, properly, and at the right time, they keep your stride fluid and reduce injuries. Don't, however, confuse these stretching exercises with warming up. Stretching, or static activities, should be done as part of the cool-down. Warm-up is a dynamic activity and should be done before you run.

Warm-Up

A dynamic, or movement-based, warm-up is most effective. Static stretching before a workout can reduce muscle power during the workout. A warm-up increases the temperature in and blood flow to the muscles you will use during your workout. A dynamic warm-up will protect you against injury and make your muscle contractions more efficient.

None of the warm-up or cool-down exercises require body contact with the ground. You can do all the movements standing up. I have found that, because of the various weather conditions runners encounter, staying off the ground during the warm-up and cool-down promotes a consistent routine and reduces the chance for illness.

The best way to warm up before running is to start by briefly walking and then moving on to a slow run. Finish the warm-up run at a little faster pace. If your workout is more vigorous, you might want to do simple dynamic exercises like jumping jacks, arm swings, alternating toe touches, and four-count toe touches.

JUMPING JACK

Stand straight with legs together and arms at your sides (a). While jumping, spread the legs wide and reach the hands overhead (b). Return to the original position, with feet together and arms at your sides. Do one set of 10 to 15 repetitions.

ARM SWING

Stand up straight with arms at your sides. Swing your arms forward in a big circle for 10 repetitions (a-b), and then swing them backward for 10 repetitions. Do one set.

ALTERNATING TOE TOUCH

Stand up straight with your legs spread a little wider than shoulder width and your arms outstretched to the sides and parallel to the ground (a). Bend forward and touch your right foot with your left hand (b), and then straighten up to the starting position. Bend forward and touch your right hand to your left foot and return to the starting position. Do one set of 10 repetitions.

FOUR-COUNT TOE TOUCH

Stand straight up with your arms at your sides. Bend over and touch your toes. In one motion, straighten up and lightly hit your abdomen with your fists, and then do an easy jump while raising your arms over your head. When your feet hit the ground, bring your arms down and again lightly hit your abdomen with your fists. Repeat the movement. Do one set of 10 repetitions.

Depending on the workout, you might want to run strides just before the workout starts. If you plan to do a longer, steady run, you can incorporate the warm-up into that mileage by running easily for the first mile or two.

In addition to raising your temperature and increasing your blood flow, a warm-up provides another benefit: your body will talk to you during the warm-up. "Listen to your body" is good advice. Listening, however, isn't always enough. You must also know how to analyze what your body is telling you. Sometimes what the body and mind tell you needs further clarification. One of these times is before your workout. This need for clarification is another reason the warm-up period is important.

Examples of Messages That Need Clarification

1. Let's say you're an early-morning runner. You wake up stiff and tired in the chilly predawn. You think to yourself that you are in no shape to run and that your body is telling you to take a day off.
2. Perhaps you're a late-afternoon runner. A minor injury has interfered with your recent runs, but you don't notice it as you move through your day. You think you've recovered and are ready to resume running.
3. You could be facing a big race. Your anxiety has you feeling weak and doubtful. You don't believe you have the strength to get to the starting line.

In each of these examples, clarification will help you decide how to proceed. If you believe everything your body and mind are indicating, you could make a mistake. You might not run on a morning that could rejuvenate you. You might ignore a minor injury in the afternoon and turn it into a major one. Or you might let prerace nerves erode your confidence, performance, and enjoyment.

Here's where the warm-up comes in. Besides preparing you physically for training, this phase of your workout clarifies what the body and mind are saying. A warm-up tells you whether you're able to run on that cold morning. It can ease aches that you thought were serious, or it can uncover those you tried to ignore. It can modify your doubts and get you to the starting line, enabling you to mentally get into the race soon after the starting gun goes off with a greater sense of confidence.

By the time you've warmed up, your body and mind will be telling the truth. Imaginary or transient problems will have eased, if not vanished, and real concerns will still be there, if not intensified. After you've warmed up, listen closely to your body and believe what it says.

Initial Cool-Down

After a workout, you need to give your body a chance to return to a normal resting state over time. You don't want to do this instantaneously. Actually, you should look at the cool-down as your first step in the recovery process. The worst thing you can do now is jump into your car and drive home. Don't even sit down. Keep moving.

During a workout your muscle cells have probably experienced micro-trauma and the debris from that trauma, small as it might be, needs to be removed from the muscle cell and moved into the blood stream. If you stop cold turkey, the blood flow through the muscle cells decreases too quickly, leaving significant amounts of debris in the cells. This can intensify the normal and required inflammation process that occurs every time you work out and can impede the recovery process.

Begin the cool down with easy running immediately after you finish your workout. Then you may walk a little until your pulse and breathing rates descend gradually toward normal.

The apparent air temperature rises about 20 degrees Fahrenheit (nearly 10° C) while you're running. This will drop rapidly as soon as you stop. If the day is even a little chilly or if there is a cool breeze, your body's temperature will also drop rapidly and you'll feel chilled. This condition enhances your chances of becoming ill. It is believed that becoming chilled constricts the blood vessels in the nose, decreasing the blood low that supplies the white cells that fight infection. If a person encounters a virus at this time, the reduction of defenses makes it more difficult to fight the virus and common cold symptoms may develop. Thus some people who would otherwise have fought off the virus without becoming symptomatic fall ill as a consequence of experiencing a chill. Rather than increasing your chance of illness, be prepared to exchange your sweaty or damp clothes for dry ones before the next cool-down step. Add extra clothing or layers if you'll be outside for long. Now you're ready for the next cool-down step, stretching.

Static Stretching During Cool-Down

Running by its nature is a tightening activity. It reduces the flexibility all over, from shoulders to feet. If left uncorrected, this tightness sets you up for soreness and injury. Stretching counteracts the inflexibility that running causes.

The muscles are most receptive to stretching when they're warm and tight, and they are least likely to be injured then by the very exercises that are supposed to prevent injury. Stretching exercises can *cause* injuries if done improperly or at the wrong time. Because the running motion is quick and jarring, therapeutic stretches must be slow and soothing. Remember to follow these three key rules of stretching:

1. Stretch slowly to the point of discomfort, but do not push or bounce into the pain zone.
2. Breathe normally—don't hold your breath.
3. Hold the exercise for several seconds at the borderline between comfort and discomfort.

Eight stretches are suggested. It should take just a little more than 5 minutes to complete all of them. I'm sure many people will say that is not enough time. But I've found that most people don't stretch if they must spend more than 5 or 6 minutes. I'd rather have you do some than none. And if you do them consistently, they will be worthwhile, even if you spend only a short time on them. If you want, you can spend more time by repeating the process, holding the stretches a little longer, or adding your own favorite stretches.

The rest of this section presents stretches to counterbalance the tightening effects that running has on the muscles. Once again, because of the weather conditions you might face and to set up a consistent pattern of stretching, no stretches take place on the ground. Also, you need no equipment or support structure such as a tree or branch. When stretching, start at the neck and work down the body to the feet.

NECK STRETCH

Stand up straight with your arms at your sides. Slowly bend the neck forward (a), backward (b), right (c), and left (d). Repeat this movement for about 30 seconds.

SHOULDER STRETCH

Stand up straight with your arms at your sides. Reach up as high as you can (a), and then bring the arms down and hug yourself (b). Drop your hands to your sides and reach backward (c). Hold each position for about 20 seconds.

ABDOMINAL STRETCH

Stand up straight with your feet about shoulder-width apart and your hands at your sides. Place your hands at the top of your buttocks. Bend comfortably backward. Hold the stretch for about 30 seconds.

BACK STRETCH

Stand up straight with your feet together and your hands at your sides. Bend forward with your hands touching or pointing toward your toes. Hold the stretch for about 20 seconds.

HIP STRETCH

Stand up straight with your feet a little wider than shoulder width and your arms at your sides. Bend forward, placing you right hand on your left elbow and your left hand on your right elbow (a). Try to get your elbows as close to the ground as you can. Hold this position for about 15 seconds, then straighten your arms and try to touch your left foot with both hands (b). Hold this position for about 15 seconds, and then try to touch your right foot with both hands (c). Return to the center position with your arms folded as before. Hold this position for about 15 seconds, and then return to a standing position.

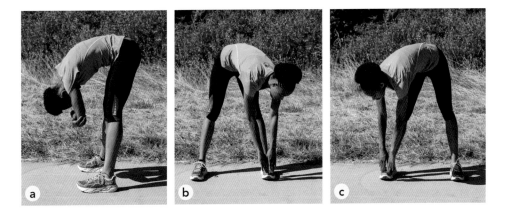

HAMSTRING STRETCH

Stand up straight with your left leg in front of your right leg and your arms at your sides *(a)*. Bend forward and touch or try to touch your toes *(b)*. Hold for about 20 seconds. Stand up and switch the position of the legs. Once again bend forward and touch or try to touch your toes. Hold this stretch for about 20 seconds and then return to the starting position.

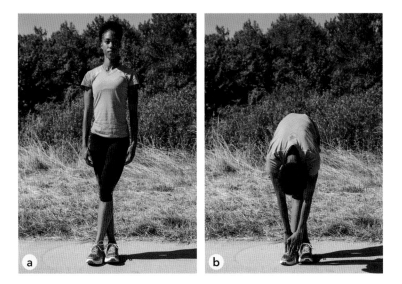

CALF STRETCH

Stand up straight. Step out with a long stride with your right foot and then move your left leg slightly back *(a)*. Bending your left leg slightly, sink so the right thigh is nearing parallel to the ground *(b)*. This will help get a deeper stretch in the calf. You can rest your arms on the right thigh if you need to. Hold this position for about 20 seconds and then switch legs and repeat for another 20 seconds.

ACHILLES AND ARCH STRETCH

Stand up straight with your arms at your sides. Move one foot forward about 12 inches (30 cm). Keeping your heel on the ground, bend the foot and toes back. Hold for about 20 seconds and then repeat with your other foot. You can perform this exercise barefoot or while wearing shoes.

Total Stretching Time: 5:20

Pre- and Postworkout Nutrition

Fueling your body is an important part of your training program. This includes preworkout and postworkout nutrition. I include this here because taking in nutrition should be part of your warm-up and cool-down down routine.

Preworkout Nutrition

Your preworkout nutrition should include protein, carbohydrate, and fluid. Protein is important because it will help inhibit the normal process of tissue breakdown during a workout and accelerate protein synthesis during recovery. Carbohydrate is important because you will use glycogen, the carbohydrate fuel stored in your cells, during the workout, and a fresh supply of carbohydrate will help prevent glycogen depletion. Fluid is important because during exercise you will lose fluid through sweating and respiration to keep the body from overheating. Although the increased energy metabolism required during exercise produces water, water loss during the same period could be 10 to 15 times greater than water production. Preworkout consumption of protein, carbohydrate, and fluid will pay dividends.

Preworkout nutrition is not difficult. Reach for a simple, effective, tasty, inexpensive, and convenient drink that provides protein, carbohydrate, and fluid. Ignore the row upon row of energy drinks. Not only do these usually contain little protein and too much sugar that spikes insulin release, most are also packed with caffeine or some form of stimulant. Caffeine can enhance results, but your body gets accustomed to it, and you eventually need more to produce the same result. It also plays havoc with your hormonal system, especially loss of adrenalin reserves. Caffeine in coffee, up to the amount that would be found in about five cups of regular coffee, is considered legal. But save it for a race, and then just one cup will do.

The preworkout drink that is ideal for everyone except people who cannot tolerate dairy is chocolate milk. This fluid contains protein and carbohydrate. Drink a glass of nonfat chocolate milk about 30 minutes before your workout. If your workout will be a longer than usual, you can also precede the milk with a piece of whole-wheat bread. As the bread is digested, it will slowly release carbohydrate, producing an increase in blood glucose without sharply raising insulin levels. You can substitute a banana for the bread if you prefer to avoid wheat products. If you would like to try a protein shake, find one that contains whey. Whey is absorbed quickly and gets to work sooner.

A whey protein drink might work well for people who are lactose intolerant, if they choose one containing whey protein concentrate or isolate whose non-protein components have been removed. Or they could take a lactase enzyme just before consuming the whey drink.

Another habit you should develop is drinking 2 to 3 cups (473-710 ml) of water during the two hours before you work out. If your run will last longer than 2 hours, make sure water is available (with you or stowed) so you can drink on the run every 3 to 4 miles (4.8-6.4 km).

Postworkout Nutrition

Postworkout nutrition is a continuation of the recovery process. And the sooner you start it after the workout, the more effective it is. Your body will again require the protein, carbohydrate, and fluid you included in your preworkout nutrition plan, but it also needs vitamins and minerals to replace those it has lost. And if your workout was a long run, your body also needs to restore unsaturated fats, known as good fats. The two most pressing requirements are to restore glycogen to the muscle cells and to accelerate protein synthesis in the muscle cell. Glycogen depletion and muscle-tissue breakdown can create performance problems if you don't address them daily.

The shelves are full of choices for postworkout nutrition. But chocolate milk remains a good choice to accomplish glycogen restoration, protein synthesis, and more. Chocolate milk is high in protein and carbohydrate. It has a high water content that helps replace the water lost through sweat and respiration. It contains minerals, including calcium that helps support bone and energy metabolism. Because it is a liquid, it is quickly absorbed into the body. And its protein-to-carbohydrate composition makes it more effective than plain milk.

Drinking chocolate milk after a workout instead of a commercial recovery drink can reduce muscle breakdown, keep glycogen concentrations high, increase lean body mass, and improve maximum oxygen consumption. You have many choices in postworkout drinks. Be sure to choose one that contains minerals, carbohydrate, and protein.

Eating a banana along with drinking milk might be your best postworkout option. Bananas contain three forms of carbohydrate: glucose, fructose, and sucrose. And they act as a time-release carbohydrate source. They also contain large amounts of potassium, a mineral used in muscle contractions and to promote bone health and fluid balance between the interior and exterior of cells and in sending nerve signals. They contain dietary fiber, which helps moderate hunger. And like milk, they are easy to digest and easily absorbed. So consider including a banana as part of your recovery process. If you don't like bananas, you can substitute a piece of bread.

Depending on the intensity of your workout, drink 8 to 16 ounces (236-478 ml) of chocolate milk and eat a banana within 30 minutes of completing the workout. Waiting longer than that decreases the effectiveness of the post-workout nutrition. If you prefer a protein shake after your workout, choose one that contains both whey and casein. Together these ingredients act as time-release amino acid sources.

Cross-Training

10

Cross-training is engaging in a physical activity that is not your primary activity. Cross-training offers a runner an alternative method of working out that can serve five major purposes:

1. Strengthen and balance muscle groups and their tendons and ligaments
2. Improve or maintain flexibility
3. Provide a mental break from running
4. Substitute other activities for running on easy or rest days
5. Maintain fitness during periods of injury

You have many options for cross-training activities. You can go to a gym to lift weights, take an exercise class, or use aerobic equipment. Or if you prefer, you can perform most of those activities at home. You can follow your favorite running courses on a bike or inline skates or head out to explore new neighborhoods. Each of these activities meets one or more of the five purposes of cross-training. However, perhaps your best option is working out in the water because it meets all five criteria.

Water Workouts

This section focuses on using water to reduce the effects of gravity while you are in a vertical position and moving in a running motion. A flotation device can help keep you vertical and buoyant and allows you to work on proper form. Although some people don't use a flotation device, frequently their focus shifts to keeping their head above water and their form suffers. Your workout can be as strenuous with a device as without. And you get the added benefit of developing good form. You can also do water aerobics or swim. In addition to helping heal injuries, water exercise is effective for recovery and overall body conditioning.

The use of water for training and rehab has a long and documented history. The Romans built baths in 60 A.D., and Bath, England, is named for the warm, soothing baths that were developed there. In the 1930s an

Australian nurse known as Sister Kenny pioneered the use of water in the rehabilitation of polio patients; her treatment quickly proved less painful and more effective than other protocols. In the 1960s heavyweight boxing champion Muhammad Ali used water for training. And race horse trainers usually include water running in their training and recovery regimens.

What makes water a good medium for cross-training and rehabilitation? Water has weight. It is much heavier than air. This causes pressure, called hydrostatic pressure, to increase as the depth increases. At rest, the pressure is equal at all parts of the body. But when parts of the body move, pressure increases against the direction of the movement creating resistance. This resistance to movement is similar to the resistance provided by weight training and builds strength.

Water has drag. Drag is the difference between front and back pressure. As you move a straight arm through the water there is more pressure in front of the arm than behind it. That is drag. Eddies, which impede flow, are also created, and this adds more resistance. The faster the limb moves through the water, the greater the resistance.

Water has viscosity. Water molecules are attracted to each other, and this attraction induces friction and causes more resistance.

Water has buoyancy. The density of the body is greater than the density of the water. For this reason, the body sinks until the weight of the water displaced equals the weight of the body. The weight of the body in water is about 10 percent of its weight on land. Buoyancy counteracts the pull of gravity and makes moving injured limbs through the water easier and less painful.

weight of a body in water = body weight on land − weight of displaced water

Water has specific heat. Specific heat is the heat required to raise the temperature of a substance 1 degree Centigrade. The specific heat of water is 25 times the specific heat of air, so the body will conserve water because of the cooling effects of water. This results in less sweating.

So water provides resistance, in both muscles that promote movement and those that oppose movement, creating a better balance between muscle groups. Water allows you to work in a gravity-free environment. And water keeps the body cooler. (See table 10.1 for water's benefits.)

Table 10.1 Benefits Water Provides to a Healthy Runner

Relaxes the body
Improves flexibility and range of motion
Promotes recovery of joints and antigravity muscles
Provides an alternative environment for aerobic training
Enables training partners to communicate while in the water
Works synergistic and antagonistic muscle groups at the same time, which promotes strength and balance

If you are a healthy runner using water as an optional workout, just follow the parameters set out for the workout scheduled: same duration and perceived intensity. Water workouts are especially suited for easy days because you complete the workout while giving your body a chance to recover. Remember the pre- and postworkout nutrition is important just when working out in the water.

If you want to swim, use the standard strokes, preferably the crawl. But swimming is a solitary endeavor. Some runners, accustomed to looking around and talking with friends as they run, think of pool workouts as sensory deprivation. In that case water aerobics is another possibility.

If you are working out in the water because you are injured, remember these three rules regarding injury:

1. While working on range of motion, stay behind the point of pain. For example, if you are bending your knee and the pain starts at 20 degrees, don't bend it beyond 21 degrees.
2. Nudge the range of motion and intensity; don't force them.
3. When the injury starts feeling better, don't do anything foolish. Keep your return to normal training time gradual.

The next step in your recovery is to continue the water workouts while adding walking or jogging in the shallow end and then easy walking and jogging on grass. (See table 10.2 for benefits of water workouts for an injured runner.)

Table 10.2   Benefits Water Provides to an Injured Runner

Eliminates impact
Starts rehabilitation earlier
Provides a safe environment in which to rehab
Increases range of motion to the injured area
Alleviates pain through easier movement
Increases circulation to the injured area
Mobilizes edema from the injured area
Reeducates neuromuscular patterns
Reduces atrophy in injured area
Speeds return to on-ground training

Aerobic Workouts in the Gym

You have two options for an aerobic workout in the gym: equipment or classes. The most commonly used equipment includes the treadmill, elliptical trainer, stationary bike, and the rowing machine. Many types of aerobic dance, exercise, and movement classes are available in a range of levels from low impact and relatively easy to highly challenging. This organized group activity is a great option for people who like company when they exercise. If you choose one of these options, beware of high-impact routines and movements that your body might be unfamiliar with and could cause injury. Warm up well and do a little less than you think you can handle rather than more, even when you are being urged on by the class leader.

Aerobic Workouts at Home

Much of the equipment you find in the gym, you can purchase for your home. Although the machines are somewhat expensive, treadmills, rowing machines, and elliptical trainers made for home use are cheaper than those made for the gym. Less expensive home workout options include aerobic exercise and dance videos, television shows, and a basic jump rope.

If you want to train outdoors, consider a bicycle, elliptical trainer made for the road, or a Kickbike. Kickbikes are human-powered scooters with a frontend that resembles a bicycle. Inline skates and skateboards offer an aerobic workout but are a little more risky for less coordinated runners.

Bicycling is popular with runners for many of the same reasons running is. It takes them outdoors on the same routes they would travel as runners and lets them explore twice as much territory as they could on foot.

Walking delivers only about one-third the pounding of running. You can walk anywhere, anytime, and with very little risk of developing impact ailments. But because walking is such an efficient exercise, workouts tend to be low intensity. The benefits come more slowly than they do with running and other cross-training activities, and you must walk a longer time to cover the same distance to achieve those benefits. But the real benefit of walking is that it is a relaxing and low-key activity that contrasts nicely with your challenging running workouts. And you can walk with family and friends, or even your dog.

Strength Training With Body-Weight Exercises

There are so many options for strength training that you might feel overwhelmed. And a variety of apps promise hundreds of exercises. However, if you prefer to follow the philosophy of this book and keep it simple, I present just a few basic strength exercises you can use to improve your overall fitness.

Strength training is not usually a cross-training activity that you do to take a break. You use it to improve and balance your overall body strength. Because running is a one-directional action, it builds some muscles more than others. Strength imbalances can occur, and these can lead to injuries. Strength exercises can restore and maintain muscle balance. These can be as simple as body-weight exercises or as complex as a formal weight-training workout in a gym with a personal trainer. Tried-and-true body-weight exercises include push-ups, sit-ups, half squats, bouncing, and burpees.

Table 10.3 lists a basic, but worthwhile, 10-exercise, body-weight routine. You can perform these exercises two or three times a week. And try to do them on a harder running day, after the run and before the stretching. Why? You continue to gain aerobic conditioning. You are warmed up. You can reserve your easy days to emphasize recovery.

You can vary the exercises, reps, and progression, but once again, stick to simple exercises that feel right to you. Don't do an exercise if it causes injury or pain.

Table 10.3   Basic Body-Weight Exercises

Exercise	Body region worked	Reps	Progression*
Bounce	Calves and feet	25	2
Sit-up	Core	20	2
Push-up	Arms and shoulders	12	1
Plank	Core	3 × 10 sec	1
Knee to chest	Legs	12 each	1
Burpee	Whole body	6	1
Toe raise	Calves and feet	20	2
Superman	Low back	8	1
Triceps dip	Arms and shoulders	10	1
Toe flex	Feet	20 sec per foot	No change

*Number of repetitions to add per month

BOUNCE

Stand up straight with your arms at your sides *(a)*. Relax your knees and bounce gently on your toes *(b)*. Do one set of 25 reps.

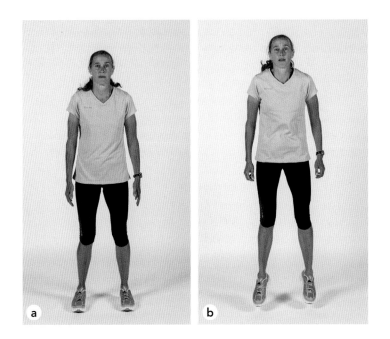

SIT-UP

Lie on your back on the floor. Place your hands on your chest. Bend your legs slightly and keep your feet flat on the floor or hook them under a stable object *(a)*. Contract the abdominal muscles to sit up so your trunk is at about a 45-degree or 90-degree angle with the floor *(b)*. Do one set of 20 reps.

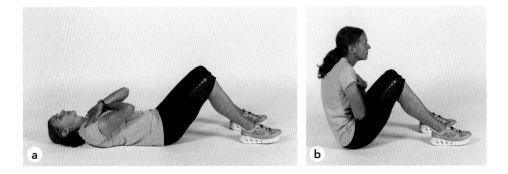

PUSH-UP

Kneel on the floor. Lean forward and place your hands under your shoulders. Straighten your legs so the toes touch the ground *(a)*. Bend your arms so your chest and chin touch the floor *(b)*. Don't bend your head forward. Your head, back, and legs should make a straight line. Do one set of 12 reps.

You can also do this exercise from a kneeling position, keeping your head and back in a straight line as you bend your elbows and bring your chest and chin to the floor. Then straighten your arms and return to the starting position.

PLANK

Kneel on the floor. Lean forward and place your elbows and forearms on the floor under your shoulders. Straighten your legs so the toes are touching the ground. Don't bend your neck. Your head, back, and legs should make a straight line. Hold the position for 3 sets of 10 seconds.

KNEE TO CHEST

Stand up straight, with your feet together and your arms at your sides. To prepare, bend your knees slightly (a). Then jump up, bending your legs and bringing the knees up to so the thighs are approximately parallel to the floor (b). Landing lightly on the balls of your feet, stand straight and repeat. Do one set of 12 repetitions. If you have trouble doing 12 reps in a row, split them into smaller sets and gradually increase the number of repetitions per set.

BURPEE

Stand straight with your legs together and your arms extended straight over your head (a). As you do a deep-knee bend, place your hands on the ground under your shoulders (b) and straighten your legs and place your toes on the ground assuming a push-up position (c). Then bring your knees under your body again (d) and return to the standing position (e). Do 1 set of 6 repetitions.

TOE RAISE

Stand up straight with your feet together and your hands at your sides (a). Raise your heels off the floor so only the toes remain in contact (b). Then return the heels to the floor. Repeat. Place your hands on a wall, chair, or bannister for support, if necessary. Do 1 set of 20 repetitions.

SUPERMAN

Lie facedown, with your arms straight out in front of your body and your legs straight behind you (a). Simultaneously raise your arms, chest, and legs off the floor (b). Then return to the starting position. Do 1 set of 8 repetitions.

TRICEPS DIP

Sit on the floor with your knees bent, your heels on the ground, and your arms bent with the palms on the floor, fingers facing forward *(a)*. Straighten your arms to raise your buttocks off the floor *(b)*, and then return to the starting position. Do 1 set of 10 repetitions.

TOE FLEX

Seated on a chair or bench, place your heels on the floor, and bend the foot up. Curl your toes forward. Hold that position for 20 seconds.

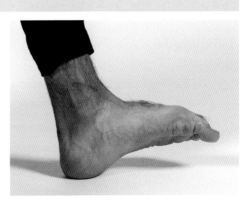

When you finish the entire routine, you can top it off with about 2 minutes of dumbbell running, moving your arms like you would when you run. The weight should be just 5 or 10 pounds (3-5 kg) per dumbbell. After that, if you have a bar, a bar hang for about 20 seconds will help your body stretch out. Next do a stationary stand on each leg for 3 sets of 10 seconds to develop your balance. Then take 10 belly breaths, inhaling slowly and deeply. Finish with your usual postworkout stretching and nutrition.

This basic program may be too easy or too hard for you, especially at first. You are not limited to it. Do more or fewer exercises. Use more or less weight. Do more or fewer reps. Make it fit your level of fitness and your personal goals. But if in doubt, always go easier rather than harder. You can do more after you've learned how your body reacts to the challenge.

Strength-training equipment for the home covers a wide range of possibilities. Dumbbells, barbells, and resistance bands have been around for a long time because they have proven effective. Stretching bands or cords are becoming popular because they work the whole body and are easy to take on trips. Large exercise balls can be used for multiple exercises and can even serve as a foundation for bench presses and sit-ups.

Yoga has been used for centuries in the Far East and is now popular throughout the world. Depending on the positions you select and how long you hold them, yoga can improve physical flexibility and strength as well as mental concentration. It is an ideal way to improve breathing, an important aspect of running, and to promote relaxation and recovery.

Strength Training With Equipment

If you go to a gym, you can choose from many types of strength-promoting equipment, including free weights and almost any type of machine using any type of movement you can imagine. Table 10.4 lists 10 basic movements you can do with free weights, dumbbells, or machines. Exercise instructions and illustrations are included following the table. Practice the motion you will use in the exercise five or six times without weight before you start each exercise.

Table 10.4   Basic Exercises With Equipment

Exercise	Area worked	% body weight	Reps	Progression*
Upright row	Arms and chest	25	8	1
Leg curl	Hamstrings	12.5	8	1
Leg extension	Quadriceps	12.5	8	1
Bench press	Arms and chest	25	8	1
Bench sit-up	Core	No weight	20	2
Split press	Arms and chest	20	12	1
Hanging knee raise	Core	No weight	15	1
Bent-leg deadlift	Low back	33	8	1
Clean and press	Arms and core	25	8	1
Chin-up or pull-down	Arms and chest	Chin-up: no weight Pull-down: 50	Chin-up: total max + 2 in 2 sets Pull-down: 2 sets of 6	Retest max

*Number of repetitions to add per month

UPRIGHT ROW

Select dumbbells or a bar that is the appropriate weight. Bring the weight off the floor so it is in front of the body and your arms are straight *(a)*. If using a bar, grip the bar so that the hands are 3 or 4 inches (7.6-10 cm) apart and bring it up to your chin *(b)*. If you're using dumbbells, lift the weight to your chest. Return the weight to the starting position. Do 1 set of 8 repetitions.

LEG CURL

Put an appropriate weight on the weight bar. Lie facedown on a leg curl bench and place your ankles under the footpads *(a)*. Bend the knees and lift the weight until the lower legs are perpendicular to the floor *(b)*. Return your legs to the starting position. Do 1 set of 8 reps.

LEG EXTENSION

Put an appropriate weight on the weight bar. Sit on the leg-extension bench, bend your knees, and place your lower shins under the pads *(a)*. Straighten the legs and lift the weight until the legs are parallel to the floor *(b)*. Return to the starting position. Do 1 set of 8 repetitions.

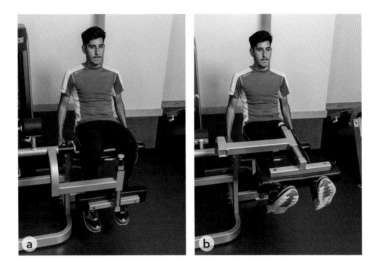

BENCH PRESS

Select an appropriate weight. Place it on the weight bench standards or have someone place the weight in your hands after you are in position. While lying on the bench grasp the bar with your arms about shoulder-width apart and lower it to your chest *(a)*. Straighten your arms to raise the bar *(b)*. Return the bar to the starting position. When you finish, replace the bar on the bench standards or have someone take the bar out of your hands. Do *not* attempt to sit up while holding the bar. Do 1 set of 8 repetitions.

BENCH SIT-UP

Sit on the incline bench with your feet under the footpads. Lie back and place your hands behind your head or across your chest *(a)*. Raise your trunk so that it is at a 45- to 90-degree angle to the floor *(b)*. Return to the starting position. Do 1 set of 20 repetitions.

SPLIT PRESS

Select an appropriate weight. With the barbell in front of your feet, slightly bend your knees. Bend over and squat slightly and grasp the barbell with your hands about shoulder-width apart. Straighten your knees and trunk and bring the barbell up to your lower abdomen and then up to your chest *(a)*. Lift the barbell over your head, simultaneously straightening your arms and jumping slightly, bringing one leg back a few inches and the other leg forward a few inches *(b)*. Bring the barbell back down to your lower abdomen and repeat, but this time reverse the position of the legs. Continue, alternating the position of the feet with each repetition. Do 1 set of 12 repetitions. When finished, lower the bar to the abdomen and perform a slight squat to return the barbell to the floor.

HANGING KNEE RAISE

Jump up and grasp the chinning bar with your hands about shoulder-width apart (a). While hanging, bring your knees up toward your chest (b). Return to the starting position. Do 1 set of 15 repetitions.

BENT-LEG DEADLIFT

Select an appropriate weight. Stand with the barbell in front of your feet and slightly bend your knees. Bend over into a slight squat and grasp the barbell with the hands about shoulder-width apart (a). Rise to a standing position with arms and legs straight and the barbell at about thigh level (b). With knees slightly bent, bend at the waist until your upper body is almost parallel to the floor (c). Then straighten to the standing position. Repeat. Do 1 set of 8 repetitions

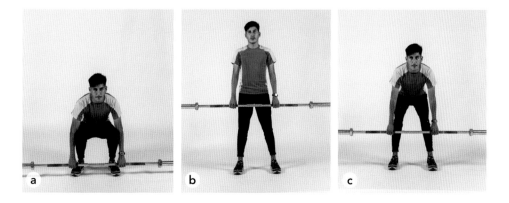

CLEAN AND PRESS

Select an appropriate weight. With the barbell in front of your feet, slightly bend your knees. Bend over, squat slightly, and grasp the barbell with your hands about shoulder-width apart (a). Perform the following actions in three distinct steps, taking only a slight break between steps:

1. Straighten your knees and trunk, bringing the barbell up to your lower abdomen, while maintaining the squat position.
2. Then extend the legs and bring the barbell up to your chest (b).
3. Straighten your arms to lift the barbell overhead (c).

Reverse the steps to return to the starting position. Repeat the movement sequence. Do 1 set of 8 repetitions.

CHIN-UP OR PULL-DOWN

Chin-up: Jump up and grasp the bar with your hands about shoulder-width apart *(a)*. Hang straight and then pull yourself up so the chin is over the bar *(b)*. Lower yourself until your arms are straight. Repeat the movement. Perform 2 sets that total the maximum number of reps you can do in 1 set plus 2 more repetitions. For example, if your max per set is 6, do 2 sets of 4 reps for a total of 8. If your maximum per set is less than 5, do the pull-down instead.

Pull-down: Select an appropriate weight. (Start with half your body weight and gradually add weight over time.) Sitting under the pull-down bar, reach up and grasp the bar with arms straight and hands about shoulder-width apart *(a)*. Pull the bar down under your chin *(b)*, then return to the starting position. Do 2 sets of 6 for a total of 12 repetitions.

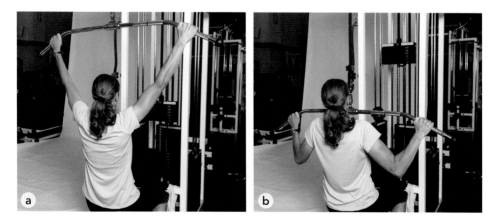

Stretching in the Shower

The shower might seem like a strange place to do cross-training. But it's the perfect place to practice belly breathing and do three stretches. Belly breathing helps you transport and consume oxygen more efficiently. It also helps you stay more relaxed during the critical parts of a competition. The three stretches that follow reinforce flexibility in three key areas of the body. And doing them in a warm environment makes the muscles and tendons more receptive. For safety reasons, do these exercises only in a shower with a nonslip floor.

WALL LEAN FOR THE CALVES AND ARCHES

Stand about 30 inches (76 cm) from the shower wall, with your palms on the wall. Lean forward, keeping your body straight, until your head almost touches the wall. Hold the position for 30 to 45 seconds.

BACK ARCH FOR THE CHEST AND ABDOMEN

Stand up straight with your feet about shoulder-with apart and your hands at your sides. Place your hands at the top of your buttocks and bend comfortably backward. Hold the stretch for 30 to 45 seconds.

HANGING TOE TOUCH FOR THE LOW BACK

Stand up straight with your feet together and your hands at your sides. Bend forward with your hands touching or pointing toward your toes. Hold the stretch for 30 to 45 seconds.

Cross-training can help you maintain fitness while you recover from an injury. It can also improve your strength and flexibility and inject variety into your training program to keep it fresh.

Runner's Diary

11

As we've seen in earlier chapters, people run for a variety of reasons and enjoy the physical and emotional benefits it offers. If you, too, want to reap these benefits, you have to stay with it. Running is an endurance activity, to be sure, but its benefits have a limited life span. Stop for as little as a month and the benefits begin to dwindle, but keep running and they constantly improve. So your main goal is to be consistent. I want you to be out there running—enjoying it and profiting from it—for a lifetime. This is winning in the truest sense. Regardless of how fast or how far you go, in running you win by lasting—and by outlasting—those who get injured or lose interest and burn out or drop out. Winners make running a part of their lives!

Despite the ease of putting numbers to running results, for most runners the greatest value of running isn't measured in numbers. More important is the feeling, the exhilaration of putting in solid efforts and then enjoying well-earned rest and relaxation afterward. It's the knowledge that you can keep going and the desire to keep coming back for more. That said, it's only natural to want to know how you're doing.

Evaluating Your Progress

Whatever your goal is in running, you have precise ways to measure your progress toward it. Running is imminently measurable. You work with the objective standards of distance and time.

For example, if your goal is to increase the distance of your longest run or your total weekly distance, you know you've done it as soon as you add laps around the track or extend your road course. If your goal is to run a certain distance faster than before or to improve your overall pace, you know you've succeeded as soon as you look at your watch and check the time.

Maybe your goals are more personal. They might be centered less on how far and fast you run and more on how running makes you feel and look. Your feedback might come from your mirror, your scale, the way your clothes fit, or an internal sensation that you are toned, strong, and rested.

You might run to keep your cardiovascular system in shape to boost your energy and endurance throughout the day. You can tell how effectively you're training this system by checking your resting pulse rate for the stronger, slower beats you're seeking.

Whether you prefer to focus more closely on the numbers or the physical and emotional signs, you want to see progress. Changes in performance results and physical signals do occur. They come to almost everyone at almost any age and any initial state of fitness who takes an honest, consistent approach to running. But these changes don't come instantly—not overnight, not in a week, and not even in as long as a month. These are long-term reactions as the body slowly adapts to the work asked of it. Progress comes on its own schedule.

Along the way, you want to know that you're on the right track and to keep an eye out for obstacles. You want to see where you're going and where you've been. This is where the runner's diary comes in.

Most other sports keep diaries of some kind, too, because they provide a way to evaluate progress and to enhance performance. Basketball teams track shooting and scoring percentages from every area of the court in various game scenarios. Football teams track the effectiveness of defensive and offensive schemes against each opponent they face, game in and game out. They can cite numbers for how effective they are at home and on the road, on grass and synthetic surfaces. Baseball teams track batting averages, slugging percentages, and on-base percentages. They can provide pitching performance statistics such as earned run average.

Running is a simple sport. And in keeping with the theme of this book, we're going to keep it simple.

Benefits of Keeping a Running Diary

Like health and fitness, running is a lifetime endeavor. A season from now, a year from now, a decade from now—you can look back proudly at how far you've progressed. But where do you look? You can look in the records you keep. We recommend that you keep a diary, journal, or log of your workouts. That way, you capture two of running's beauties: its measurability and comparability.

Distance, time, weight, and pulse are all quickly and easily measured. By writing them down today, you'll be able to compare them accurately with what you achieve in the near and distant future. Then you'll know exactly how far you have traveled.

Perhaps the most important reason to keep a diary is to monitor data regarding sickness and injury. The diary can help you understand why an illness or injury might have occurred or tip you off that you are at risk for one or the other. Lack of sleep is the cause of many illnesses, as is overtraining. Watching your diary for early signs of sleeping too little or training too much can help you stay healthy.

Your personal accounting can be as simple as a notation on a calendar or in a notebook. Or it can be as sophisticated as one of the published diaries or computer applications available commercially for this purpose. You might jot down a few quick numbers. Or you might add words of commentary about the experience. Where and how you keep your records doesn't matter. Just be sure to keep them consistently and to cover the essentials.

Knowing where you've been can be as important as planning where you're going. Keeping a running diary enables you to get to know yourself better. You can track what works well for you and what doesn't. You can learn from your mistakes and avoid repeating them.

Your running diary can help you

- chart your progress,
- develop and maintain effective training habits,
- understand how a problem may have developed,
- monitor your rehabilitation, and
- reinforce your commitment.

A sample diary that you can print and complete each week is available at www.humankinetics.com/products/all-products/Fitness-Running-3rd -Edition. Keep the pages in a binder for easy reference. At the beginning of each week you can write in your suggested workouts for the week and then simply underline the ones you have completed or modified each time you run. There is also space for comments. You can see a completed sample at the end of this chapter.

You may prefer to track your running information using some other format, perhaps using a program on your phone or tablet. Use whatever type of diary works best for you. Comments that describe mood, health, and potential injury status are especially helpful.

What to Include in Your Diary Entries

Write down the workouts for the week. Underline the workouts you completed and make comments about them. At the very least, underline the total time it took to complete the workout and estimate the distance.

Other factors you might include are the pace per mile or kilometer, terrain, weather conditions, and how you felt both physically and mentally. Be sure to include information regarding pain, discomfort, or injuries. You can make your short comments below the workout information. Include anything that seems relevant to your physical and emotional state, such as a change in your daily schedule or a trip. Some people like to rate these factors on a numeric scale, say 1 to 10. Others use words like "great" or "very tired." You could even draw simple pictures that illustrate your mood, a frowning or smiling face.

Pay special attention to the harder workouts. These are the intervals, steady states, fartleks, tempo runs, out and backs, and races that give the best indications of your performance. Compare them with previous workouts of the same type. For example, if an out and back two weeks ago took 30 minutes to complete and yesterday's, over the same course, took 29:15, you know you're improving.

Also listen carefully to your body. It's telling you how your training is going. Get in the habit of recording your resting pulse as you wake up each morning and recording it in your running diary. A lower reading over time means that your cardiovascular fitness is improving. If you notice a sudden jump of 5 beats or more in your heart rate, it could mean that you're overtraining and need a rest. Know what your norm is so you can act when it changes.

Also, record your weight each morning. Most runners expect to experience some long-term weight loss or at least to maintain their weight and not to gain. But a sudden drop of 3 percent isn't a good sign. Again, it could signal that you've exceeded optimum training, and a break is needed.

There is no right or wrong way to use a diary. The important thing is to use one as you see fit.

Sample Training Log

Here is a completed sample weekly diary page for someone preparing to run a 5K race. The runner's current best time at this distance is 23:57, for an estimated $\dot{V}O_2$max of 42. The goal, based on a $\dot{V}O_2$max of 44, is 23:00—for a goal pace of 7:25 per mile (4:36/km). Maximum duration for this person is 60 minutes. HR means morning heart rate. BW means morning body weight taken nude, after using the toilet and before eating. HS means a subjective rough guess of how many hours you slept.

Table 11.1 Sample Completed Training Log

Program 5K		Week 12			Date 9/28/15		Goal			
Day	Workout (priority)	Duration	% $\dot{V}O_2$max	Pace per mile		Distance	HR	BW	HS	
Sunday	Long (1)	42 min	60-70	10:07- 11:48		4 miles	62	155	7.5	
Monday	Recovery (5)	30 min	50-60	11:48-14:09		2.5 miles	60	154	8	
Tuesday	Race prep (3)	4 × mile	Goal pace, "miles felt smooth"	7:30 7:25 7:25 7:20		4 miles plus warm-up and cool-down	63	155	7	
Wednesday	Recovery (5)	30 min	50-60	11:48-14:09		2.5 miles	65	153	8.5	
Thursday	Interval (2)	6 × 400 m	100, "1:38 for last 400 was nice"	1:45 1:42 1:40 1:40 1:42 1:38		1.5 miles plus warm-up and cool-down	61	154	8	
Friday	Recovery (7)	30 min	50-60	11:48-14:09		2.5 miles	60	155	8.5	
Saturday	Recovery (4)	30 min	50-60	11:48-14:09		3 miles	59	156	7.5	

PART III

Training Schedules

Here comes the payoff. You're ready to take the individual ingredients of training, mix them together, and take the workouts to the road, track, and trail. It's time to bring those numbers to life.

The programs here are based on your abilities and your goals. Of course, over time your performance level and goals will change. As your fitness improves and your desire to explore this sport grows, you can update your training schedule to match your new abilities and goals. We offer programs for six areas of emphasis:

1. Beginning training (chapter 12): Use this program if you want to start running to improve your fitness level or resume after a lengthy pause.

2. Fitness training (chapter 13): Use this program if you run and walk or run for exercise for relatively short distances and at relaxed paces.

3. Short-race training (chapter 14): Use this program not only to prepare for running a faster mile or 1,500 meters but also for 5K to 12K races.

4. Half marathon training (chapter 15): Use this program to prepare for a race from 15K to 25K.

5. Marathon training (chapter 16): Use this program to train for the marathon and for intermediate races such as 30K and 20 miles.

6. Postrace recovery and injury training (chapter 17): Use this program to recover from a race, an injury, or an illness. You can also use it to get back on track if you have been training too hard.

Beginning Training

How do you start running if this is your first try at a formal program or if you're trying again after a lengthy pause? Begin by walking. "You must walk before you run" is a truism that applies to this activity as well as to many other endeavors in the wider world.

Walk is not a bad four-letter word—or a sign of weakness or surrender. Walking is simply a point on a continuum stretching between strolling at one extreme and sprinting at the other. Walking benefits runners in many ways—it works well as a warm-up or cool-down for running, as a recovery break during interval training, as an alternative activity on rest days, and as an exercise option during injury.

The safest way to launch a *running* program is to start *walking*. Can you walk easily and painlessly for half an hour? If not, begin your fitness quest by working up to this level. Once you're walking the prerequisite 30 minutes, then you can run in small amounts, with intervals of walking in between.

Measure the walk and run intervals by minutes, not by distance. This is simpler than measuring the route you take, and it removes the pressure of having to run a particular distance at a set pace. Time yourself with a digital stopwatch, and put in a total of 30 minutes from the first day.

Run and walk three or four days a week, allowing at least one day off between sessions. On some of the *rest* days, simply walk a little or substitute another cross-training activity, such as bicycling. Go through the 10 weeks listed, decreasing the time spent walking as the time spent running increases.

All running in this program should feel comfortable, and a full week's training should feel easy before you advance. The training plans are listed by week, but listen to your body and progress at your own rate. Skip a week or more if the recommended sessions seem too easy for you; repeat a week, or even drop back in the program, as needed.

Once you can run 30 minutes steadily, you can graduate to fitness training or even short-race training. In these more advanced programs you run additional days per week and you sometimes run for more than a half hour.

"Running! If there's any activity happier, more exhilarating, more nourishing to the imagination, I can't think of what it might be. In running the mind flees with the body, the mysterious efflorescence of language seems to pulse in the brain, in rhythm with our feet and the swinging of our arms."

Joyce Carol Oates

Beginning Training: Week 1

Day	Total time	Run–walk mix	Total run
Sunday	30 min	Walk 25, run 5	5 min
Monday	Cross-train or rest		
Tuesday	30 min	Walk 25, run 5	5 min
Wednesday	Cross-train or rest		
Thursday	30 min	Walk 25, run 5	5 min
Friday	Cross-train or rest		
Saturday	30 min	Walk 25, run 5	5 min

Beginning Training: Week 2			
Day	Total time	Run–walk mix	Total run
Sunday	Cross-train or rest		
Monday	30 min	Walk 10, run 5, walk 10, run 5	10 min
Tuesday	Cross-train or rest		
Wednesday	30 min	Walk 10, run 5, walk 10, run 5	10 min
Thursday	Cross-train or rest		
Friday	30 min	Walk 10, run 5, walk 10, run 5	10 min
Saturday	Cross-train or rest		

"The ultimate winners are not the young athletes who finish first this week or this season, but those who learn early that they never want to stop."

Skip Grant

Metabolism has two parts: anabolism and catabolism. Anabolism builds up complex molecules, and catabolism breaks them down.

Beginning Training: Week 3			
Day	Total time	Run–walk mix	Total run
Sunday	30 min	Walk 20, run 10	10 min
Monday	Cross-train or rest		
Tuesday	30 min	Walk 20, run 10	10 min
Wednesday	Cross-train or rest		
Thursday	30 min	Walk 20, run 10	10 min
Friday	Cross-train or rest		
Saturday	30 min	Walk 20, run 10	10 min

Beginning Training: Week 4			
Day	Total time	Run–walk mix	Total run
Sunday	Cross-train or rest		
Monday	30 min	Walk 10, run 5, walk 5, run 10	15 min
Tuesday	Cross-train or rest		
Wednesday	30 min	Walk 10, run 5, walk 5, run 10	15 min
Thursday	Cross-train or rest		
Friday	30 min	Walk 10, run 5, walk 5, run 10	15 min
Saturday	Cross-train or rest		

Every cell has mitochondria, which serve as centers of aerobic energy production. When you train aerobically you develop more mitochondria.

For the sake of consistency, try to work out at the same time every day. Also have your running clothes laid out or packed in a sports bag waiting for you in the same place first thing each morning; this way you won't have to skip a workout because you don't have all your gear.

Beginning Training: Week 5

Day	Total time	Run–walk mix	Total run
Sunday	30 min	Walk 15, run 15	15 min
Monday	Cross-train or rest		
Tuesday	30 min	Walk 15, run 15	15 min
Wednesday	Cross-train or rest		
Thursday	30 min	Walk 15, run 15	15 min
Friday	Cross-train or rest		
Saturday	30 min	Walk 15, run 15	15 min

Beginning Training: Week 6			
Day	Total time	Run–walk mix	Total run
Sunday	Cross-train or rest		
Monday	30 min	Walk 5, run 5, walk 5, run 15	20 min
Tuesday	Cross-train or rest		
Wednesday	30 min	Walk 5, run 5, walk 5, run 15	20 min
Thursday	Cross-train or rest		
Friday	30 min	Walk 5, run 5, walk 5, run 15	20 min
Saturday	Cross-train or rest		

On cold days, wear extra clothing at the start of the workout or bring it with you. As the workout progresses and you get warmer, you can always take off some items—but you can't put them on if you don't have them with you.

When you find a pair of shoes that feel great, buy extra pairs while they are available. You can always return them if the first pair doesn't work out as well as you'd hoped. Shoe companies are always changing the design and construction, and the improvements they make could alter the very thing that made that first pair just right for you.

Beginning Training: Week 7			
Day	Total time	Run–walk mix	Total run
Sunday	30 min	Walk 10, run 20	20 min
Monday	Cross-train or rest		
Tuesday	30 min	Walk 10, run 20	20 min
Wednesday	Cross-train or rest		
Thursday	30 min	Walk 10, run 20	20 min
Friday	Cross-train or rest		
Saturday	30 min	Walk 10, run 20	20 min

Beginning Training: Week 8			
Day	Total time	Run–walk mix	Total run
Sunday	Cross-train or rest		
Monday	30 min	Run 5, walk 5, run 20	25 min
Tuesday	Cross-train or rest		
Wednesday	30 min	Run 5, walk 5, run 20	25 min
Thursday	Cross-train or rest		
Friday	30 min	Run 5, walk 5, run 20	25 min
Saturday	Cross-train or rest		

"The only discipline that lasts is self-discipline."

Bum Phillips

A diary is an important tool. When you look back, you recognize patterns that improved your performance and should be repeated and others that had a negative impact and should be avoided.

Beginning Training: Week 9

Day	Total time	Run–walk mix	Total run
Sunday	30 min	Walk 5, run 25	25 min
Monday	Cross-train or rest		
Tuesday	30 min	Walk 5, run 25	25 min
Wednesday	Cross-train or rest		
Thursday	30 min	Walk 5, run 25	25 min
Friday	Cross-train or rest		
Saturday	30 min	Walk 5, run 25	25 min

Beginning Training: Week 10			
Day	Total time	Run-walk mix	Total run
Sunday	Cross-train or rest		
Monday	30 min	Run all 30	30 min
Tuesday	Cross-train or rest		
Wednesday	30 min	Run all 30	30 min
Thursday	Cross-train or rest		
Friday	30 min	Run all 30	30 min
Saturday	Cross-train or rest		

I used to run with my dog. While I ran around the track, Misty would lie in the middle and watch. She was probably wondering why I was expending all that energy just to stay in the same place. Some days I wondered the same thing.

Fitness Training

Running purely for fitness, as opposed to training for races, is a perfectly honorable pursuit. You run for the aerobic benefits, weight control, stress management, and similar personal-fitness reasons. And you run enough to test yourself in organized fun runs up to 5K (3.1 miles), if you're so tempted.

The program outlined here lasts 13 weeks, or three months, or one season of the year. You can train three or four days each week, depending on your other time commitments for the week. The priority numbers indicate a workout's order of importance with 1 being the most important and 7 being the least. When you run fewer days than seven, drop workouts starting from the highest number (7) and work downward. Determine the appropriate duration and pace of your runs according to the tables in chapter 7, Program Setup. Take this information and plug it into the training formulas provided for each week.

Some suggestions offer a range for paces. Select what feels right for you on a particular day. You don't always have to go for the fastest pace. Consistency of training is more important than always testing yourself.

For tempo or out-and-back workouts (starting in week 4), add a warm-up of a 5- to 6-minute run and 4 × 50-meter strides. Also add a cool-down run of 3 to 5 minutes. (Refer to chapter 9 for more information on warm-up and cool-down options.)

"If you don't think you were born to run you're not only denying history, you're denying who you are."

Christopher McDougall

Fitness Training: Week 1

Day	Workout (priority)	Duration	Pace	% $\dot{V}O_2max$
Su	Long (1)	Max time	Moderate	60-70
M	Recovery (5)	1/2 max time	Easy	50-60
Tu	Recovery (4)	1/2 max time	Easy	50-60
W	Steady state or fartlek (2)	2/3 max time	SWS	75-85
Th	Recovery (7)	1/2 max time	Easy	50-60
F	Steady state or fartlek (3)	2/3 max time	SWS	75-85
Sa	Recovery (6)	1/2 max time	Easy	50-60

		Fitness Training: Week 2			
Day	Workout (priority)	Duration	Pace	% $\dot{V}O_2$max
Su	Long (1)	Max + 1 min	Moderate	60-70
M	Recovery (5)	1/2 max time	Easy	50-60
Tu	Recovery (4)	1/2 max time	Easy	50-60
W	Steady state or fartlek (2)	2/3 max + 1 min	SWS	75-85
Th	Recovery (7)	1/2 max time	Easy	50-60
F	Steady state or fartlek (3)	2/3 max time	SWS	75-85
Sa	Recovery (6)	1/2 max time	Easy	50-60

"In running, it doesn't matter whether you come in first, in the middle of the pack, or last. You can say, 'I have finished.' There is a lot of satisfaction in that."

Fred Lebow

> "Train, don't strain."
>
> Arthur Lydiard

Fitness Training: Week 3

Day	Workout (priority)	Duration	Pace	% $\dot{V}O_2$max
Su	Long (1)	Max + 2 min	Moderate	60-70
M	Recovery (5)	1/2 max time	Easy	50-60
Tu	Recovery (4)	1/2 max time	Easy	50-60
W	Steady state or fartlek (2)	2/3 max + 2 min	SWS	75-85
Th	Recovery (7)	1/2 max time	Easy	50-60
F	Steady state or fartlek (3)	2/3 max time	SWS	75-85
Sa	Recovery (6)	1/4 to 1/2 max	Easy	50-60

Fitness Training: Week 4				
Day	Workout (priority)	Duration	Pace	% $\dot{V}O_2$max
Su	Tempo or out and back (1)	1/2 max time	SWS to strong	85-95
M	Recovery (5)	1/2 max time	Easy	50-60
Tu	Recovery (3)	1/2 max time	Easy	50-60
W	Recovery (7)	1/2 max time	Easy	50-60
Th	Steady state or fartlek (2)	2/3 max + 3 min	SWS	75-85
F	Recovery (6)	1/2 max time	Easy	50-60
Sa	Recovery (4)	1/2 max time	Easy	50-60

"Encourage kids to enjoy running and play in athletics. Don't force them to run too much competition."

Arthur Lydiard

You can't do a 100 percent effort for 20 minutes. If you did, your muscle proteins would start to resemble hard-boiled eggs.

		Fitness Training: Week 5		
Day	Workout (priority)	Duration	Pace	% $\dot{V}O_2max$
Su	Long (1)	Max + 3 min	Moderate	60-70
M	Recovery (5)	1/2 max time	Easy	50-60
Tu	Recovery (4)	1/2 max time	Easy	50-60
W	Steady state or fartlek (2)	2/3 max + 4 min	SWS	75-85
Th	Recovery (7)	1/2 max time	Easy	50-60
F	Steady state or fartlek (3)	2/3 max time	SWS	75-85
Sa	Recovery (6)	1/2 max time	Easy	50-60

	Fitness Training: Week 6			
Day	Workout (priority)	Duration	Pace	% $\dot{V}O_2$max
Su	Long (1)	Max + 4 min	Moderate	60-70
M	Recovery (5)	1/2 max time	Easy	50-60
Tu	Recovery (4)	1/2 max time	Easy	50-60
W	Steady state or fartlek (2)	2/3 max + 5 min	SWS	75-85
Th	Recovery (7)	1/2 max time	Easy	50-60
F	Steady state or fartlek (3)	2/3 max time	SWS	75-85
Sa	Recovery (6)	1/2 max time	Easy	50-60

Mostly we track calories, but that's only a small part of a much bigger picture. What we need to track are the factors that increase energy resources: rest, diet, and exercise.

The cilia in the throat and upper bronchial tubes move debris up and out of the lungs. They like a warm environment because it enhances blood flow. Wear a turtle-neck dickey on cold days to keep the lower neck and upper bronchial area warm.

		Fitness Training: Week 7		
Day	Workout (priority)	Duration	Pace	% $\dot{V}O_2$max
Su	Long (1)	Max + 5 min	Moderate	60-70
M	Recovery (5)	1/2 max time	Easy	50-60
Tu	Recovery (4)	1/2 max time	Easy	50-60
W	Steady state or fartlek (2)	2/3 max + 6 min	SWS	75-85
Th	Recovery (7)	1/2 max time	Easy	50-60
F	Steady state or fartlek (3)	2/3 max time	SWS	75-85
Sa	Recovery (6)	1/4 to 1/2 max	Easy	50-60

Fitness Training: Week 8

Day	Workout (priority)	Duration	Pace	% $\dot{V}O_2$max
Su	Tempo or out and back (1)	1/2 max time	SWS to strong	85-95
M	Recovery (5)	1/2 max time	Easy	50-60
Tu	Recovery (3)	1/2 max time	Easy	50-60
W	Recovery (7)	1/2 max time	Easy	50-60
Th	Steady state or fartlek (2)	2/3 max + 6 min	SWS	75-85
F	Recovery (6)	1/2 max time	Easy	50-60
Sa	Recovery (4)	1/4 to 1/2 max	Easy	50-60

Don't complain about the weather. Others have to deal with the same conditions you do. I advised a runner who regularly complained about it, especially the wind, to become one with the weather. She embraced the suggestion and henceforth looked forward to whatever weather Mother Nature sprung on her. It gave her an advantage.

When you run, thinking of a few key words or a phrase can help you improve your form. Here are some suggestions:

- Fingers: relaxed and slightly bent
- Shoulders: parallel to the ground and loose, not hunched
- Tall: upright and aligned
- Belly breathe: the abdomen goes out when you inhale and in when you exhale.

Fitness Training: Week 9

Day	Workout (priority)	Duration	Pace	% $\dot{V}O_2$max
Su	Long (1)	Max + 6 min	Moderate	60-70
M	Recovery (5)	1/2 max time	Easy	50-60
Tu	Recovery (4)	1/2 max time	Easy	50-60
W	Steady state or fartlek (2)	2/3 max + 6 min	SWS	75-85
Th	Recovery (7)	1/2 max time	Easy	50-60
F	Steady state or fartlek (3)	2/3 max time	SWS	75-85
Sa	Recovery (6)	1/2 max time	Easy	50-60

		Fitness Training: Week 10		
Day	Workout (priority)	Duration	Pace	% $\dot{V}O_2$max
Su	Long (1)	Max + 7 min	Moderate	60-70
M	Recovery (5)	1/2 max time	Easy	50-60
Tu	Recovery (4)	1/2 max time	Easy	50-60
W	Steady state or fartlek (2)	2/3 max + 6 min	SWS	75-85
Th	Recovery (7)	1/2 max time	Easy	50-60
F	Steady state or fartlek (3)	2/3 max time	SWS	75-85
Sa	Recovery (6)	1/2 max time	Easy	50-60

A high school athlete set a goal to win the 800 meters at the state championships. Her coach asked her to run the 1,500 as well. Over the two-day meet, the stress of qualifying rounds and the 1,500 final, in which she placed second, caused significant pain in her lower leg, probably shin splints. With her sights still set on her goal of an 800-meter victory, she taped the leg and ran a disciplined race behind the leaders until the last 100 meters. From there she made her move and passed her competition in the last 5 meters. She honored her goal not only for the race, but for the whole year.

Some runs are harder than others, even though you are going at the same pace. It is helpful to imagine that you feel the same way you do on a good day, even if you aren't running as fast or as efficiently as you do on a good day.

Fitness Training: Week 11

Day	Workout (priority)	Duration	Pace	% $\dot{V}O_2max$
Su	Long (1)	Max + 8 min	Moderate	60-70
M	Recovery (5)	1/2 max time	Easy	50-60
Tu	Recovery (4)	1/2 max time	Easy	50-60
W	Steady state or fartlek (2)	2/3 max + 6 min	SWS	75-85
Th	Recovery (7)	1/2 max time	Easy	50-60
F	Steady state or fartlek (3)	2/3 max time	SWS	75-85
Sa	Recovery (6)	1/2 max time	Easy	50-60

Fitness Training: Week 12

Day	Workout (priority)	Duration	Pace	% $\dot{V}O_2max$
Su	Tempo or out and back (1)	1/2 max time	SWS to strong	85-95
M	Recovery (5)	1/2 max time	Easy	50-60
Tu	Recovery (3)	1/2 max time	Easy	50-60
W	Recovery (7)	1/2 max time	Easy	50-60
Th	Steady state or fartlek (2)	2/3 max + 6 min	SWS	75-85
F	Recovery (6)	1/2 max time	Easy	50-60
Sa	Recovery (4)	1/2 max time	Easy	50-60

I once knew a runner who routinely became so upset before a race that she wanted to leave the track and skip the race. She and her coach worked through her anxiety by taking one step at a time. Her prerace warm-up involved a six-step pattern. She and her coach made a pact that they would pause after each step and decide whether to take the next step. Facing each step individually and knowing that she could choose not to continue kept her from feeling overwhelmed and got her to the starting line. Once the event began, she usually ran a very good race.

Mary Slaney was very nervous as we flew into Helsinki for the 1983 World Championships. She said she couldn't get the races out of her head. I asked her to focus completely on the races for 10 minutes twice a day and then let it go—watch TV, do laundry, take a walk. I told her that if she allowed herself to be anxious about the races for longer than that, she would deplete her adrenalin. She followed my advice to perfection and remained calm, noting that the other runners seemed very uptight in comparison.

Fitness Training: Week 13

Day	Workout (priority)	Duration	Pace	% $\dot{V}O_2$max
Su	Steady state or fartlek (2)	2/3 max + 7 min	SWS	75-85
M	Recovery (4)	1/4 max time	Easy	50-60
Tu	Recovery (7)	1/4 max time	Easy	50-60
W	Steady state or fartlek (3)	2/3 max + 7 min	SWS	75-85
Th	Recovery (5)	1/4 max time	Easy	50-60
F	Recovery (6)	1/4 max time	Easy	50-60
Sa	Long (1)	Max + 10 min	Moderate	60-70

Short-Race Training

Short is a relative term. To someone whose daily run ends at a half hour or less, a race of 30 to 60 minutes doesn't sound *short*. Or when you run all out for even 1 mile or 1.5 kilometers, the distance doesn't feel *short*.

The distances we discuss in this chapter are short compared to other road races. They're the shortest events that a distance runner will race—1,500 meters or 1 mile on the track, and 5K to 10K on the track, road, or a cross country course. The 5K and 10K runs are the most common road race distances.

When someone who doesn't run hears you are a runner, the first question is likely to be, "How fast do you run a mile?" This is true even in many countries that use the metric system to measure distance. The mile and its metric versions, 1,500 and 1,600 meters, are track's most popular races.

The 5K carries different meanings to different groups of runners. On the track it goes by the name 5,000 meters. The 5K is a common cross country distance in high school. Mostly it's a road distance and the race length that draws the greatest number of runners. Even here you find variety. The 5K serves as an entry point for new racers and also as a place where experienced runners race their fastest.

When mass-participation road racing grew in the 1970s and 1980s in the US and Europe, the 10K spurred much of that growth. It was the street version of track's 10,000 meters. This is the distance of such classic races as Peachtree in Atlanta, Georgia, which started with 4,000 runners and now caps the number of participants at 60,000, and Bolder Boulder in Colorado, which started with 2,000 runners and now draws 50,000 participants. The slightly longer 12K events, such as Bay to Breakers in San Francisco, California, with 110,000 participants, and the Lilac Bloomsday race in Spokane, Washington, with 50,000 runners, are also quite popular.

The program outlined here lasts 13 weeks, or three months, or one season of the year. The priority numbers indicate a workout's order of importance with 1 being the most important and 7 being the least. When you run fewer days than seven, drop workouts starting with the highest number (7) and work downward. Determine the appropriate durations and paces of your runs using the tables in chapter 7, Program Setup. Take this information and plug it into the training formulas provided for each week.

Some suggestions offer a range for paces. Select what feels right for you on a particular day. You don't always have to go for the fastest pace. Consistency of training is more important than always testing yourself.

For tempo or out-and-back workouts (starting in week 4), add a warm-up of a 5- to 6-minute easy run and 4 × 50-meter strides. Also add a cool-down easy run of 3 to 5 minutes. Refer to chapter 9 for more information on warm-up and cool-down options.

For all repetition-type workouts (strides, intervals, speed, race-preparation), follow the faster segment with a slower one of equal length (for example, 4 × 400 meters with a 400-meter recovery run and walk between each). If you choose to do new interval training, roll on at a slower pace than the interval but faster than a jog.

When you train for goal-pace runs, select a pace that corresponds to your $\dot{V}O_2$max plus 2 points. For example, a runner with a current reading of 50 has a goal-pace $\dot{V}O_2$max of 52.

	Short-Race Training: Week 1			
Day	Workout (priority)	Duration	Pace	% $\dot{V}O_2$max
Su	Long (1)	Max time	Moderate	60-70
M	Recovery (5)	1/2 max time	Easy	50-60
Tu	Speed (4)	5 × 100 m	Strong	90-100
W	Steady state or fartlek (2)	2/3 max time	SWS	75-85
Th	Recovery (7)	1/2 max time	Easy	50-60
F	Steady state or fartlek (3)	2/3 max time	SWS	75-85
Sa	Recovery (6)	1/2 max time	Easy	50-60

"As every runner knows, running is about more than just putting one foot in front of the other; it is about our lifestyle and who we are."

Joan Benoit Samuelson

"Winning has nothing to do with racing. Most days don't have races anyway. Winning is about struggle and effort and optimism, and never, ever, ever giving up."

Amby Burfoot

Short-Race Training: Week 2

Day	Workout (priority)	Duration	Pace	% $\dot{V}O_2max$
Su	Long (1)	Max + 2 to 4 min	Moderate	60-70
M	Recovery (5)	1/2 max time	Easy	50-60
Tu	Speed (4)	7-8 × 100 m	Strong	90-100
W	Steady state or fartlek (2)	2/3 max + 1 to 2 min	SWS	75-85
Th	Recovery (7)	1/2 max time	Easy	50-60
F	Steady state or fartlek (3)	2/3 max time	SWS	75-85
Sa	Recovery (6)	1/2 max time	Easy	50-60

Short-Race Training: Week 3				
Day	Workout (priority)	Duration	Pace	% $\dot{V}O_2$max
Su	Long (1)	Max + 4 to 6 min	Moderate	60-70
M	Recovery (5)	1/2 max time	Easy	50-60
Tu	Speed (4)	4-6 × 200 m	Strong	90-100
W	Steady state or fartlek (2)	2/3 max + 2 to 3 min	SWS	75-85
Th	Recovery (7)	1/2 max time	Easy	50-60
F	Steady state or fartlek (3)	2/3 max time	SWS	75-85
Sa	Recovery (6)	1/4 to 1/2 max	Easy	50-60

Visualization is effective. Images fire neurons just like actions fire neurons. There is a personal highlight film in your brain, and you can revisit it. Also you can create new images. Doing it two or three days before the race is ok, but there is no need to do it more than twice a day and no need to do it for more than 10 minutes.

Monitoring your physical status and energy level can help you decide how hard you should train on a particular day. If you have not recovered from your previous efforts, plan an easier day or take the day off.

	Short-Race Training: Week 4			
Day	Workout (priority)	Duration	Pace	% $\dot{V}O_2$max
Su	Tempo or out and back (1)	1/2 max time	SWS to strong	85-95
M	Recovery (5)	1/2 max time	Easy	50-60
Tu	Interval or new interval (3)	3 to 5 × 300 m	Strong	90-100
W	Recovery (7)	1/2 max time	Easy	50-60
Th	Steady state or fartlek (2)	2/3 max + 2 to 4 min	SWS	75-85
F	Recovery (6)	1/2 max time	Easy	50-60
Sa	Speed (4)	7 to 10 × 100 m	Strong	90-100

		Short-Race Training: Week 5			
Day	Workout (priority)	Duration	Pace	% $\dot{V}O_2$max	
Su	Long (1)	Max + 6 to 8 min	Moderate	60-70	
M	Recovery (5)	1/2 max time	Easy	50-60	
Tu	Speed (4)	8 to 10 × 100 m	Strong	90-100	
W	Steady state or fartlek (2)	2/3 max + 3 to 5 min	SWS	75-85	
Th	Recovery (7)	1/2 max time	Easy	50-60	
F	Steady state or fartlek (3)	2/3 max time	SWS	75-85	
Sa	Recovery (6)	1/2 max time	Easy	50-60	

"The idea that the harder you work, the better you're going to be is just garbage. The greatest improvement is made by the man or woman who works most intelligently."

Bill Bowerman

Percy Cerutty was the coach of Herb Elliott, who won the 1,500-meter race at the 1960 Rome Olympics. The night before the final, Percy took Herb to a track and ran a 1,500 for him. He said, "Herb, you can run faster but you can't run harder." A trait of many good coaches is that they have to set an example and do what they ask their athletes to do.

Short-Race Training: Week 6

Day	Workout (priority)	Duration	Pace	% $\dot{V}O_2$max
Su	Long (1)	Max + 8 to 10 min	Moderate	60-70
M	Recovery (5)	1/2 max time	Easy	50-60
Tu	Speed (4)	10 × 100 m	Strong	90-100
W	Steady state or fartlek (2)	2/3 max + 4 to 6 min	SWS	75-85
Th	Recovery (7)	1/2 max time	Easy	50-60
F	Steady state or fartlek (3)	2/3 max time	SWS	75-85
Sa	Recovery (6)	1/2 max time	Easy	50-60

| \multicolumn{5}{c}{Short-Race Training: Week 7} |
Day	Workout (priority)	Duration	Pace	% $\dot{V}O_2$max
Su	Long (1)	Max + 10 to 12 min	Moderate	60-70
M	Recovery (5)	1/2 max time	Easy	50-60
Tu	Interval or new interval (4)	6 to 10 × 200 m	Strong	90-100
W	Steady state or fartlek (2)	2/3 max + 4 to 6 min	SWS	75-85
Th	Recovery (7)	1/2 max time	Easy	50-60
F	Steady state or fartlek (3)	2/3 max time	SWS	75-85
Sa	Recovery (6)	1/4 to 1/2 max	Easy	50-60

When I took an athlete I was going to coach to see Bill Bowerman, he would always point his finger at them and say in a fairly fierce voice, "Is running fun? If it isn't, don't do it!"

The fight-or-flight response is the body's reaction to feeling threatened or challenged, a feeling you might face during a hard practice session or your goal race. It provides an energy boost so you can meet the situation. Sometimes it's better to fight. Sometimes it's better to flee. The one thing you don't want to do is overuse the fight-or-flight response. In today's world, we manufacture stressors that call upon the response needlessly. Save it for the real thing.

Short-Race Training: Week 8

Day	Workout (priority)	Duration	Pace	% $\dot{V}O_2$max
Su	Tempo or out and back (1)	1/2 max time	SWS to strong	85-95
M	Recovery (5)	1/2 max time	Easy	50-60
Tu	Interval or new interval (3)	5 to 7 × 300 m	Strong	90-100
W	Recovery (7)	1/2 max time	Easy	50-60
Th	Steady state or fartlek (2)	2/3 max + 4 to 6 min	SWS	75-85
F	Recovery (6)	1/2 max time	Easy	50-60
Sa	Speed (4)	10 × 100 m	Strong	90-100

Short-Race Training: Week 9

Day	Workout (priority)	Duration	Pace	% $\dot{V}O_2max$
Su	Long (1)	Max + 11 to 14 min	Moderate	60-70
M	Recovery (5)	1/2 max time	Easy	50-60
Tu	Interval or new interval (2)	4-6 × 400 m	Strong	90-100
W	Recovery (7)	1/2 max time	Easy	50-60
Th	Interval or new interval (3)	8 to 10 × 200 m	Strong	90-100
F	Recovery (6)	1/2 max time	Easy	50-60
Sa	Speed (4)	10 to 12 × 100 m	Strong	90-100

Your recovery indicators are abnormal and indicate you have not recovered from recent stressors, physical or emotional. You have a hard workout planned. What should you do with respect to the workout?

Remember to bring dry clothes to change into after sweating a lot or working out in the rain. Changing promptly helps the body fight off colds and infections, and it just makes you feel better.

Short-Race Training: Week 10

Day	Workout (priority)	Duration	Pace	% $\dot{V}O_2$max
Su	Tempo or out and back (1)	1/2 max time	SWS to strong	85-95
M	Recovery (5)	1/2 max time	Easy	50-60
Tu	Interval or new interval (3)	5 to 8 × 400 m	Strong	90-100
W	Recovery (7)	1/2 max time	Easy	50-60
Th	Steady state or fartlek (2)	2/3 max + 5 to 7 min	SWS	75-85
F	Recovery (6)	1/2 max time	Easy	50-60
Sa	Speed (4)	10 to 12 × 100 m	Strong	90-100

Short-Race Training: Week 11

Day	Workout (priority)	Duration	Pace	% $\dot{V}O_2$max
Su	Race prep (2)	3 × 1 mile*	Goal pace	90
M	Recovery (5)	1/2 max time	Easy	50-60
Tu	Race prep (3)	6 × 800 m*	Goal pace	90
W	Recovery (6)	1/2 max time	Easy	50-60
Th	Interval or new interval (1)	5 to 8 × 200 m	Strong	90-100
F	Recovery (7)	1/2 max time	Easy	50-60
Sa	Recovery (4)	1/2 max time	Easy	50-60

*If goal race = mile or 1500 m, then distance = 800 or 400 m

Before a prerace warm-up, let your mind wander and take a moment to enjoy your surroundings. When you start your warm-up, begin your focus. Sharpen your focus as you progress through the warm-up so that by the time you get to the starting line, the race is the only thing on your mind.

Try to keep your preworkout and prerace warm-ups as similar as possible. This helps you feel comfortable, especially before a race, because you sense you have been there before.

Short-Race Training: Week 12

Day	Workout (priority)	Duration	Pace	% $\dot{V}O_2$max
Su	Long (1)	1/2 max + 12 min	Moderate	60-70
M	Recovery (5)	1/2 max time	Easy	50-60
Tu	Race prep (3)	3 to 4 × 1 mile*	Goal pace	90
W	Recovery (6)	1/2 max time	Easy	50-60
Th	Interval or new interval (2)	6 × 400 m	Strong	90-100
F	Recovery (7)	1/2 max time	Easy	50-60
Sa	Recovery (4)	1/2 max time	Easy	50-60

*If goal race = mile or 1500 m, then distance = 800 m

Short-Race Training: Week 13

Day	Workout (priority)	Duration	Pace	% $\dot{V}O_2max$
Su	Steady state or fartlek (2)	2/3 max + 5 min	SWS	75-85
M	Recovery (4)	1/4 max time	Easy	50-60
Tu	Recovery (7)	1/4 max time	Easy	50-60
W	Speed (3)	8 × 100 m	Strong	90-100
Th	Recovery (5)	1/4 max time	Easy	50-60
F	Recovery (6)	1/4 max time	Easy	50-60
Sa	Race (1)	Race	Goal pace	100

Divide the race into six equal parts. Start at your goal pace, knowing that if you only had to run the first four parts you could do it easily and not be overly tired. The hard part comes when you hit the fifth section, the point where you have already run about 66 percent and still have 33 percent left. The key is to push yourself to stay on goal pace through this part. The physical and mental boost you get as you enter the sixth and final part still on pace helps carry you through.

Half Marathon Training

15

In all but its name, the half marathon is a perfectly wonderful event. It is a true race, not a survival test (as the marathon can become), and its training isn't like taking on a second job (as marathon preparation sometimes seems). But it shouldn't be called the half. It isn't a cut-rate version of a marathon, but a unique race with its own requirements and rewards.

This program, which also prepares you for races in the 15K to 25K range, lasts 18 weeks, or a little over four months. Train four to five days each week if you're a casual racer, and train for five to seven days if advanced. Priority numbers indicate the workouts' order of importance, with priority 1 being the most important, 7 the least. When you run fewer than seven days, drop workouts starting from the highest number (7) and work downward. Determine the appropriate durations and paces of your runs using the tables in chapter 7, Program Setup. Take this information and plug it into the training formulas provided for each week.

Some suggestions offer a range for paces. Select what feels right for you on a particular day. You don't always have to go for the fastest pace. Consistency of training is more important than always testing yourself.

For tempo or out-and-back workouts (starting in week 3), add a warm-up of a 5- to 6-minute easy run and 4 × 50-meter strides. Also add a cool-down easy run of 3 to 5 minutes. Refer to chapter 9 for more detailed information on warming up and cooling down.

Some weeks you get to choose between an out-and-back and a tempo run. If you decide to do an out-and-back run, use the same duration and intensity as the previous out and back. The tempo run can be either a 40-minute run at a somewhat strong to strong effort or a 5K to 10K race for fun. Note that long-run training runs peak at 120 minutes in these programs. If you reach that level, *do not go higher*.

For all repetition-type workouts (strides, intervals, speed, race-preparation), follow the faster segment with a slower one of equal length (for example, 4 × 400 meters with a 400-meter recovery run and walk between each). If you choose to do new interval training, roll on at a slower pace than the interval, but faster than a jog.

When you train for goal-pace runs, select a pace that corresponds to your $\dot{V}O_2$max plus 2 points. For example, if you have a current reading of 50, you'd select a goal-pace $\dot{V}O_2$max of 52.

"You have to wonder at times what you're doing out there. Over the years, I've given myself a thousand reasons to keep running, but it always comes back to where it started. It comes down to self-satisfaction and a sense of achievement."

Steve Prefontaine

Half Marathon Training: Week 1

Day	Workout (priority)	Duration	Pace	% $\dot{V}O_2$max
Su	Recovery (4)	1/2 max time	Easy	50-60
M	Steady state or fartlek (1)	2/3 max time	SWS	75-85
Tu	Recovery (5)	1/2 max time	Easy	50-60
W	Steady state or fartlek (2)	2/3 max time	SWS	75-85
Th	Recovery (6)	1/2 max time	Easy	50-60
F	Steady state or fartlek (3)	2/3 max time	SWS	75-85
Sa	Recovery (7)	1/2 max time	Easy	50-60

Half Marathon Training: Week 2

Day	Workout (priority)	Duration	Pace	% $\dot{V}O_2max$
Su	Long (1)	Max time	Moderate	60-70
M	Recovery (4)	1/2 max time	Easy	50-60
Tu	Recovery (6)	1/2 max time	Easy	50-60
W	Race prep (3)	3 × 1 mile	Goal pace	90
Th	Recovery (5)	1/2 max	Easy	50-60
F	Steady state or fartlek (2)	2/3 max + 1 min	SWS	75-85
Sa	Speed (7)	5 × 100 m	Strong	90-110

As commitment increases, perception of difficulty decreases; obstacles are just hurdles to be overcome on your way to your goal; setbacks are opportunities to learn and improve.

To improve, you should continually shuttle between mastery of a skill and taking the right level of risk at the right time: Mastery plus risk-taking yields a new level of performance.

- Taking a risk without mastery promotes panic.
- Achieving mastery but avoiding risk is really boring.

Half Marathon Training: Week 3

Day	Workout (priority)	Duration	Pace	% $\dot{V}O_2max$
Su	Long (1)	Max + 5 min	Moderate	60-70
M	Recovery (5)	1/2 max time	Easy	50-60
Tu	Speed (4)	5 × 100 m	Strong	90-110
W	Steady state or fartlek (3)	2/3 max + 2 min	SWS	75-85
Th	Recovery (7)	1/2 max time	Easy	50-60
F	Recovery (6)	1/2 max time	Easy	50-60
Sa	Tempo or out and back (2)	1/2 max	SWS to strong	85-95

Half Marathon Training: Week 4

Day	Workout (priority)	Duration	Pace	% $\dot{V}O_2max$
Su	Recovery (4)	1/2 max + 2 min	Easy	50-60
M	Steady state or fartlek (1)	2/3 max + 3 min	SWS	75-85
Tu	Recovery (5)	1/2 max + 2 min	Easy	50-60
W	Steady state or fartlek (2)	2/3 max + 3 min	SWS	75-85
Th	Recovery (6)	1/2 max + 2 min	Easy	50-60
F	Steady state or fartlek (3)	2/3 max + 3 min	SWS	75-85
Sa	Recovery (7)	1/2 max + 2 min	Easy	50-60

If you are going to make a mistake, remember it is better to undertrain than overtrain. If you undertrain, you still have adrenalin to fall back on. If you overtrain, you will have exhausted your adrenalin stores and probably set yourself up for illness or injury.

While speed is an important component of running, other aspects of training are more compatible with the half marathon training. When you train above 85 percent of $\dot{V}O_2max$, the energy converted also produces lactic acid. Some of it is recycled via lactate, and some accumulates as lactic acid. Lactic acid changes the pH of the cell and can slow the energy conversion process. It can produce what runners call the "gorilla on the back" syndrome. So be judicious in deciding when to train over 85 percent, and make it at a time when it counts.

Half Marathon Training: Week 5

Day	Workout (priority)	Duration	Pace	% $\dot{V}O_2max$
Su	Long (1)	Max + 10 min	Moderate	60-70
M	Recovery (4)	1/2 max + 2 min	Easy	50-60
Tu	Recovery (6)	1/2 max + 2 min	Easy	50-60
W	Race prep (3)	4 × 1 mile	Goal pace	90
Th	Recovery (7)	1/2 max + 2 min	Easy	50-60
F	Steady state or fartlek (2)	2/3 max + 3 min	SWS	75-85
Sa	Speed (5)	6 × 100 m	Strong	90-110

Half Marathon Training: Week 6				
Day	Workout (priority)	Duration	Pace	% $\dot{V}O_2$max
Su	Long (1)	Max + 15 min	Moderate	60-70
M	Recovery (6)	1/2 max + 2 min	Easy	50-60
Tu	Speed (4)	6 × 100 m	Strong	90-110
W	Steady state or fartlek (3)	2/3 max + 3 min	SWS	75-85
Th	Recovery (7)	1/2 max + 2 min	Easy	50-60
F	Recovery (5)	1/4 max time	Easy	50-60
Sa	Tempo or out and back (2)	1/2 max	SWS to strong	85-95

It is important to know that every cell in the body converts energy the same way. Here is the path:

- Food
- Glycolysis
- Krebs cycle
- Electron transport chain
- Oxidative phosphorylation
- Adenosine triphosphate
- Oxygen
- $ATP + H_2O + CO_2$

"There's one rule of thumb that suggests that you need one day of recovery for every mile run in a race."

Hal Higdon

Half Marathon Training: Week 7

Day	Workout (priority)	Duration	Pace	% $\dot{V}O_2$max
Su	Recovery (4)	1/2 max + 4 min	Easy	50-60
M	Steady state or fartlek (1)	2/3 max + 6 min	SWS	75-85
Tu	Recovery (5)	1/2 max + 4 min	Easy	50-60
W	Steady state or fartlek (2)	2/3 max + 6 min	SWS	75-85
Th	Recovery (6)	1/2 max + 4 min	Easy	50-60
F	Steady state or fartlek (3)	2/3 max + 6 min	SWS	75-85
Sa	Recovery (7)	1/2 max + 4 min	Easy	50-60

Half Marathon Training: Week 8

Day	Workout (priority)	Duration	Pace	% $\dot{V}O_2$max
Su	Long (1)	Max + 20 min	Moderate	60-70
M	Recovery (4)	1/2 max + 4 min	Easy	50-60
Tu	Recovery (6)	1/2 max + 4 min	Easy	50-60
W	Race prep (3)	5 × 1 mile	Goal pace	90
Th	Recovery (5)	1/2 max + 4 min	Easy	50-60
F	Steady state or fartlek (2)	2/3 max + 6 min	SWS	75-85
Sa	Speed (7)	6 × 150 m	Strong	90-110

Periodically remind yourself that challenge and recovery must be balanced between the alarm phase and the adaptation phase or your body resources will decline, and you will shift into the exhaustion phase.

To honor your goal, if possible, your day should include the following:

- Getting up at the same time
- Eating a breakfast to provide energy for the day
- Eating a healthy snack
- Eating a nutritious lunch, followed by a short period of relaxation
- Fueling your workout with preworkout nutrition
- Wearing the appropriate clothes
- Warming up properly
- Doing the workout as suggested, or doing less
- Replacing fluids, calories, and nutrients with a post-workout snack or drink
- Eating a good dinner
- Going to bed at the same time

Half Marathon Training: Week 9

Day	Workout (priority)	Duration	Pace	% $\dot{V}O_2max$
Su	Long (1)	Max + 25 min	Moderate	60-70
M	Recovery (6)	1/2 max + 4 min	Easy	50-60
Tu	Speed (4)	6 × 100 m	Strong	90-110
W	Steady state or fartlek (3)	2/3 max + 6 min	SWS	75-85
Th	Recovery (7)	1/2 max + 4 min	Easy	50-60
F	Steady state or fartlek (5)	1/4 max time	Easy	50-60
Sa	Tempo or out and back (2)	1/2 max	SWS to Strong	85-95

Half Marathon Training: Week 10				
Day	Workout (priority)	Duration	Pace	% $\dot{V}O_2$max
Su	Recovery (4)	1/2 max + 6 min	Easy	50-60
M	Steady state or fartlek (1)	2/3 max + 8 min	SWS	75-85
Tu	Recovery (5)	1/2 max + 6 min	Easy	50-60
W	Steady state or fartlek (2)	2/3 max + 8 min	SWS	75-85
Th	Recovery (6)	1/2 max + 6 min	Easy	50-60
F	Steady state or fartlek (3)	2/3 max + 8 min	SWS	75-85
Sa	Recovery (7)	1/2 max + 6 min	Easy	50-60

If you are using an altitude tent when you sleep, keep it set for 7,200 feet (about 2,900 meters). This is the altitude that provides maximal development of extra red blood cells.

> "The footing was really atrocious. I loved it. I really like cross country; you're one with the mud."
>
> Lynn Jennings

		Half Marathon Training: Week 11		
Day	Workout (priority)	Duration	Pace	% V̇O₂max
Su	Long (1)	Max + 30 min	Moderate	60-70
M	Recovery (4)	1/2 max + 6 min	Easy	50-60
Tu	Recovery (6)	1/2 max + 6 min	Easy	50-60
W	Race prep (3)	6 × 1 mile	Goal pace	90
Th	Recovery (5)	1/2 max + 6 min	Easy	50-60
F	Steady state or fartlek (2)	2/3 max + 6 min	SWS	75-85
Sa	Speed (7)	6 × 150 m	Strong	90-110

Half Marathon Training: Week 12				
Day	Workout (priority)	Duration	Pace	% $\dot{V}O_2$max
Su	Long (1)	Max + 35 min	Moderate	60-70
M	Recovery (6)	1/2 max + 6 min	Easy	50-60
Tu	Speed (4)	6 × 100 m	Strong	90-110
W	Steady state or fartlek (3)	2/3 max + 8 min	SWS	75-85
Th	Recovery (7)	1/2 max + 6 min	Easy	50-60
F	Recovery (5)	1/4 max time	Easy	50-60
Sa	Tempo or out and back (2)	1/2 max	SWS to strong	85-95

You don't necessarily need to give up on a goal race because you have experienced an injury. Take your training to the water. Time and again I saw runners with injuries that prevented them from training on the ground take to the water to continue their workouts and then perform successfully in their goal race.

A shot-putter I knew in 1984 was four weeks from the U.S. Olympic Trials when an acquaintance suggested he try a new strength-building exercise for his legs. Two weeks later he ended up injuring his legs and missed the trials. Never experiment with new training procedures close to a goal performance.

Half Marathon Training: Week 13

Day	Workout (priority)	Duration	Pace	% $\dot{V}O_2$max
Su	Recovery (4)	1/2 max + 8 min	Easy	50-60
M	Steady state or fartlek (1)	2/3 max + 10 min	SWS	75-85
Tu	Recovery (5)	1/2 max + 8 min	Easy	50-60
W	Steady state or fartlek (2)	2/3 max + 10 min	SWS	75-85
Th	Recovery (6)	1/2 max + 8 min	Easy	50-60
F	Steady state or fartlek (3)	2/3 max + 10 min	SWS	75-85
Sa	Recovery (7)	1/2 max + 8 min	Easy	50-60

Half Marathon Training: Week 14

Day	Workout (priority)	Duration	Pace	% $\dot{V}O_2$max
Su	Long (1)	Max + 40 min	Moderate	60-70
M	Recovery (4)	1/2 max + 8 min	Easy	50-60
Tu	Recovery (6)	1/2 max + 8 min	Easy	50-60
W	Race prep (3)	7 × 1 mile	Goal pace	90
Th	Recovery (5)	1/2 max + 8 min	Easy	50-60
F	Steady state or fartlek (2)	2/3 max + 10 min	SWS	75-85
Sa	Interval or new interval (7)	5 × 200 m	Strong	90-100

Winning the workout is not what it is about. Consider the real experience of the most talented runner you probably never heard of. He may have been the best American in his event ever. He even won a world-class race in which he was the rabbit, but stayed in the race. But he focused on beating everybody else in workouts. When it came time for his goal race, his emotional tank was empty.

I coached an athlete in the World Championships. She made the semifinals, and it was time for her to take a risk to see whether she could make the finals. She led most of the race but was outkicked the last 600 meters and finished fourth. She not only made the finals, but more important, she learned she could run with the big dogs. After the race she said, "Now let's work on the last 600." She made the finals next year at the Olympics and finished seventh. A risk at the right time can lead to significant improvements.

Half Marathon Training: Week 15

Day	Workout (priority)	Duration	Pace	% $\dot{V}O_2max$
Su	Long (1)	Max + 45 min	Moderate	60-70
M	Recovery (6)	1/2 max + 8 min	Easy	50-60
Tu	Speed (4)	6 × 100 m	Strong	90-110
W	Steady state or fartlek (3)	2/3 max + 10 min	SWS	75-85
Th	Recovery (7)	1/2 max + 8 min	Easy	50-60
F	Recovery (5)	1/4 max time	Easy	50-60
Sa	Tempo or out and back (2)	1/2 max	SWS to strong	85-95

Half Marathon Training: Week 16

Day	Workout (priority)	Duration	Pace	% $\dot{V}O_2$max
Su	Recovery (3)	1/2 max + 4 min	Easy	50-60
M	Recovery (6)	1/2 max + 4 min	Easy	50-60
Tu	Race prep (1)	6 × 1 mile	Goal pace	90
W	Recovery (4)	1/2 max + 4 min	Easy	50-60
Th	Race prep (2)	8 × 800 m	Goal pace	90
F	Recovery (5)	1/2 max + 4 min	Easy	50-60
Sa	Recovery (7)	1/2 max + 4 min	Easy	50-60

Take full advantage of a goal race. You never know when that kind of opportunity will occur again. An athlete I know was running heats and semis and hoped to run in the final in the 3000 race at the Olympics. In the semis she apparently thought she was going to qualify easily and slowed in the last two laps. She was not an automatic qualifier and missed one of the two extra final spots by a fraction of a second.

At the World Cross Country Championships, one of our experienced runners who qualified for the team had an injury that she realized would give her a hard time. When she saw the U.S. team's placement on the starting line, she realized that if the team didn't get out fast, there would be no possibility of winning. She gathered the team and said, "When the gun goes off, follow me!" She took off very fast and got the team to the very tight turn first. The team went on to win. Without her experience and team spirit, it would not have happened.

Half Marathon Training: Week 17

Day	Workout (priority)	Duration	Pace	% $\dot{V}O_2max$
Su	Long (1)	Max + 30 min	Moderate	60-70
M	Recovery (4)	1/2 max + 4 min	Easy	50-60
Tu	Interval or new interval (2)	12 × 400 m	Strong	90-100
W	Recovery (5)	1/2 max + 4 min	Easy	50-60
Th	Race prep (3)	5 × 1 mile	Goal pace	90
F	Recovery (6)	1/2 max + 4 min	Easy	50-60
Sa	Recovery (7)	1/2 max + 4 min	Easy	50-60

Half Marathon Training: Week 18				
Day	Workout (priority)	Duration	Pace	% $\dot{V}O_2$max
Su	Steady state or fartlek (2)	2/3 max time	Moderate	60-70
M	Recovery (4)	1/2 max + 4 min	Easy	50-60
Tu	Recovery (7)	1/2 max + 4 min	Easy	50-60
W	Speed (3)	6 × 100 m	Strong	90-110
Th	Recovery (5)	1/4 max time	Easy	50-60
F	Recovery (6)	1/4 max time	Easy	50-60
Sa	Race (1)	Half marathon	Goal pace	100

Rely on your knowledge of your goal pace to go out at a pace you know you can handle for the entire distance. It may even be a little slower than the goal pace. As you get farther into the race, your body will tell you when and how to change gears.

16

Marathon Training

Marathons are hard work. They don't begin at the starting line but in the training that begins many months earlier. They take hours to run, and they end not at the finish line, but with recovery that lasts for weeks. The difficulty of the marathon is one of its attractions, and there are a half-million marathon finishers a year in the United States alone.

This program, which also prepares you for races 30K and longer, extends 26 weeks, or six months. Train four or five days each week if you're a casual racer, five to seven days if you are more advanced. Priority numbers indicate a workout's order of importance, with priority 1 being the most important, 7 the least. When you run fewer days than seven, drop workouts starting with the highest number (7) and work downward. Determine the appropriate durations and paces of your runs using the tables in chapter 7, Program Setup. Take this information and plug it into the training formulas provided for each week.

Some suggestions offer a range for paces. Select what feels right for you on a particular day. You don't always have to go for the fastest pace. Consistency of training is more important than always testing yourself.

For tempo or out-and-back workouts (starting in week 3) add a warm-up of a 5- to 6-minute easy run and 4 × 50-meter strides. Also add a cool-down easy run of 3 to 5 minutes. Refer to chapter 9 for more detailed information on warming up and cooling down.

Some weeks you get to choose between a tempo run or an out and back. On these days you could also do a 5K to 10K race for fun.

For all repetition-type workouts (strides, intervals, speed, race-preparation), follow the faster segment with a slower one of equal length (for example, 4 × 400 meters with a 400-meter recovery run and walk between each). If you choose to do new interval training, roll on at a slower pace than the interval, but faster than a jog.

When you train for goal-pace runs, select a pace that corresponds to your $\dot{V}O_2$max plus 2 points. For example, a runner with a current reading of 50 has a goal-pace $\dot{V}O_2$max of 52.

Because marathon training is longer, recovery is more important.

"We are different, in essence, from other men. If you want to win something, run 100 meters. If you want to experience something, run a marathon."

Emil Zatopek

	Marathon Training: Week 1			
Day	Workout (priority)	Duration	Pace	% $\dot{V}O_2$max
Su	Recovery (4)	1/2 max time	Easy	50-60
M	Steady state or fartlek (1)	2/3 max time	SWS	75-85
Tu	Recovery (5)	1/2 max time	Easy	50-60
W	Steady state or fartlek (2)	2/3 max time	SWS	75-85
Th	Recovery (6)	1/2 max time	Easy	50-60
F	Steady state or fartlek (3)	2/3 max time	SWS	75-85
Sa	Recovery (7)	1/2 max time	Easy	50-60

Marathon Training: Week 2				
Day	Workout (priority)	Duration	Pace	% $\dot{V}O_2$max
Su	Long (1)	Max time	Moderate	60-70
M	Recovery (4)	1/2 max time	Easy	50-60
Tu	Recovery (6)	1/2 max time	Easy	50-60
W	Race prep (3)	3 × 1 mile	Goal pace	90
Th	Recovery (5)	1/2 max	Easy	50-60
F	Steady state or fartlek (2)	2/3 max + 1 min	SWS	75-85
Sa	Speed (7)	5 × 100 m	Strong	90-110

People who perform optimally share four characteristics:

- Commitment to a goal
- Confidence in their ability
- Control over what they can control
- Courage to take the necessary risk*

*From Kriegal, R. and Kriegal, M. 1984. *The C Zone: Peak Performance Under Pressure.* New York: Anchor Press/Doubleday.

If you've pushed yourself so hard that you start to hyperventilate, breathe into a paper bag. When you hyperventilate you exhale too much carbon dioxide. Breathing into a bag lets you bring the exhaled carbon dioxide back into the body and helps to restore the balance.

Marathon Training: Week 3

Day	Workout (priority)	Duration	Pace	% $\dot{V}O_2max$
Su	Long (1)	Max + 5 min	Moderate	60-70
M	Recovery (5)	1/2 max time	Easy	50-60
Tu	Speed (4)	5 × 100 m	Strong	90-110
W	Steady state or fartlek (3)	2/3 max + 2 min	SWS	75-85
Th	Recovery (7)	1/2 max time	Easy	50-60
F	Recovery (6)	1/2 max time	Easy	50-60
Sa	Tempo or out and back (2)	1/2 max time	SWS to strong	85-95

Marathon Training: Week 4				
Day	Workout (priority)	Duration	Pace	% $\dot{V}O_2max$
Su	Recovery (4)	1/2 max + 2 min	Easy	50-60
M	Steady state or fartlek (1)	2/3 max + 3 min	SWS	75-85
Tu	Recovery (5)	1/2 max + 2 min	Easy	50-60
W	Steady state or fartlek (2)	2/3 max + 3 min	SWS	75-85
Th	Recovery (6)	1/2 max + 2 min	Easy	50-60
F	Steady state or fartlek (3)	2/3 max + 3 min	SWS	75-85
Sa	Recovery (7)	1/2 max + 2 min	Easy	50-60

pH refers to the number of hydrogen ions (H^+) in the blood. One hydrogen ion per 555 million water molecules (H_2O) equals a pH of 7.0, which is normal. Your blood is acidic when there are 10 hydrogen ions per 555 million water molecules. Your blood is basic when there are 0.1 hydrogen ions per 555 million water molecules. Homeostasis is the process that keeps the blood normal. When you get over 85 percent $\dot{V}O_2max$ your blood becomes acidic. The body likes the pH to be normal.

Cells need stability so the internal environment can stay the same. This is called homeostasis. Claude Bernard developed the concept in the 1800s. He said, "All the vital mechanisms of the body have only one object . . . preserving the constant conditions of the inner environment." Each disturbing influence calls up a compensatory activity to neutralize the disturbance. It is dynamic self-regulation.

Marathon Training: Week 5

Day	Workout (priority)	Duration	Pace	% $\dot{V}O_2$max
Su	Long (1)	Max + 10 min	Moderate	60-70
M	Recovery (4)	1/2 max + 2 min	Easy	50-60
Tu	Recovery (6)	1/2 max + 2 min	Easy	50-60
W	Race prep (3)	4 × 1 mile	Goal pace	90
Th	Recovery (5)	1/2 max + 2 min	Easy	50-60
F	Steady state or fartlek (2)	2/3 max + 3 min	SWS	75-85
Sa	Speed (7)	6 × 100 m	Strong	90-110

		Marathon Training: Week 6		
Day	Workout (priority)	Duration	Pace	% $\dot{V}O_2$max
Su	Long (1)	Max + 15 min	Moderate	60-70
M	Recovery (6)	1/2 max + 2 min	Easy	50-60
Tu	Speed (4)	6 × 100 m	Strong	90-110
W	Steady state or fartlek (3)	2/3 max + 3 min	SWS	75-85
Th	Recovery (7)	1/2 max + 2 min	Easy	50-60
F	Recovery (5)	1/4 max time	Easy	50-60
Sa	Tempo or out and back (2)	1/2 max	SWS to strong	85-95

Years ago I coached a cross-country skier. One day she ran to the grocery store and came out with two bags of groceries. She was easily able to run home with them in her arms. On the way home, she noticed a man about a block ahead running with poor form and apparently in some degree of pain. For fun she decided to try to catch him. She did, and as she passed him she realized he was one of the nation's premier runners, who had experienced persistent injuries. Rather than rest and allow his injuries to heal, he continued to run and became more and more hobbled.

The conversion of energy only occurs in the cells, so it is important to keep the cells healthy. When you eat junk, sleep poorly, and sit on your butt, you are not respecting the cells, so they won't be able to do their best for you.

Marathon Training: Week 7

Day	Workout (priority)	Duration	Pace	% $\dot{V}O_2$max
Su	Recovery (4)	1/2 max + 4 min	Easy	50-60
M	Steady state or fartlek (1)	2/3 max + 6 min	SWS	75-85
Tu	Recovery (5)	1/2 max + 4 min	Easy	50-60
W	Steady state or fartlek (2)	2/3 max + 6 min	SWS	75-85
Th	Recovery (6)	1/2 max + 4 min	Easy	50-60
F	Steady state or fartlek (3)	2/3 max + 6 min	SWS	75-85
Sa	Recovery (7)	1/2 max + 4 min	Easy	50-60

Marathon Training: Week 8				
Day	Workout (priority)	Duration	Pace	% $\dot{V}O_2max$
Su	Long (1)	Max + 20 min	Moderate	60-70
M	Recovery (4)	1/2 max + 4 min	Easy	50-60
Tu	Recovery (6)	1/2 max + 4 min	Easy	50-60
W	Race prep (3)	5 × 1 mile	Goal pace	90
Th	Recovery (5)	1/2 max + 4 min	Easy	50-60
F	Steady state or fartlek (2)	2/3 max + 6 min	SWS	75-85
Sa	Speed (7)	6 × 150 m	Strong	90-110

After a tough marathon, it is wise to take a month off from training. A US runner who placed second in a World Marathon Championship with a big personal best went right back to her training program instead of taking a break. Her enthusiasm led to overtraining, and she never raced again.

A good reason for not making coffee a daily habit is that your body won't become accustomed to caffeine. If it does become accustomed to caffeine, you need to drink more to get the same effect. If you don't drink it usually and then drink a cup (with a little cream if you want) about 15 minutes before you run a hard workout or especially a race, it will give you a legal boost.

		Marathon Training: Week 9		
Day	Workout (priority)	Duration	Pace	% $\dot{V}O_2$max
Su	Long (1)	Max + 25 min	Moderate	60-70
M	Recovery (6)	1/2 max + 4 min	Easy	50-60
Tu	Speed (4)	6 × 100 m	Strong	90-110
W	Steady state or fartlek (3)	2/3 max + 6 min	SWS	75-85
Th	Recovery (7)	1/2 max + 4 min	Easy	50-60
F	Steady state or fartlek (5)	1/4 max time	Easy	50-60
Sa	Tempo or out and back (2)	1/2 max	SWS to strong	85-95

Marathon Training: Week 10

Day	Workout (priority)	Duration	Pace	% $\dot{V}O_2max$
Su	Recovery (4)	1/2 max + 6 min	Easy	50-60
M	Steady state or fartlek (1)	2/3 max + 8 min	SWS	75-85
Tu	Recovery (5)	1/2 max + 6 min	Easy	50-60
W	Steady state or fartlek (2)	2/3 max + 8 min	SWS	75-85
Th	Recovery (6)	1/2 max + 6 min	Easy	50-60
F	Steady state or fartlek (3)	2/3 max + 8 min	SWS	75-85
Sa	Recovery (7)	1/2 max + 6 min	Easy	50-60

If you know your diet will be good for the entire day and you get hungry between meals, it's OK to eat cookies or other sweets. They are usually packed with carbohydrate, and because you are training consistently, your body may need them to keep up your glycogen stores.

For a healthy snack at any time, try a mix of walnuts, raisins, and chocolate chips.

Marathon Training: Week 11

Day	Workout (priority)	Duration	Pace	% $\dot{V}O_2$max
Su	Long (1)	Max + 30 min	Moderate	60-70
M	Recovery (4)	1/2 max + 6 min	Easy	50-60
Tu	Recovery (6)	1/2 max + 6 min	Easy	50-60
W	Race prep (3)	6 × 1 mile	Goal pace	90
Th	Recovery (5)	1/2 max + 6 min	Easy	50-60
F	Steady state or fartlek (2)	2/3 max + 6 min	SWS	75-85
Sa	Speed (7)	6 × 150 m	Strong	90-110

		Marathon Training: Week 12			
Day	Workout (priority)	Duration	Pace	% $\dot{V}O_2$max
Su	Long (1)	Max + 35 min	Moderate	60-70
M	Recovery (6)	1/2 max + 6 min	Easy	50-60
Tu	Speed (4)	6 × 100 m	Strong	90-110
W	Steady state or fartlek (3)	2/3 max + 8 min	SWS	75-85
Th	Recovery (7)	1/2 max + 6 min	Easy	50-60
F	Recovery (5)	1/4 max time	Easy	50-60
Sa	Tempo or out and back (2)	1/2 max	SWS to strong	85-95

If you are fortunate enough train at altitude before a goal race, take a week to adjust when you get to altitude by running a little shorter and a little slower and then train at your usual sea-level effort for about four and a half weeks. When you run intervals or a tempo run, use the same pace but run only about three-quarters of the normal interval distance.

"For every runner who tours the world running marathons, there are thousands who run to hear the leaves and listen to the rain, and look to the day when it is suddenly as easy as a bird in flight."

George Sheehan

Marathon Training: Week 13

Day	Workout (priority)	Duration	Pace	% $\dot{V}O_2$max
Su	Recovery (4)	1/2 max + 8 min	Easy	50-60
M	Steady state or fartlek (1)	2/3 max + 10 min	SWS	75-85
Tu	Recovery (5)	1/2 max + 8 min	Easy	50-60
W	Steady state or fartlek (2)	2/3 max + 10 min	SWS	75-85
Th	Recovery (6)	1/2 max + 8 min	Easy	50-60
F	Steady state or fartlek (3)	2/3 max + 10 min	SWS	75-85
Sa	Recovery (7)	1/2 max + 8 min	Easy	50-60

		Marathon Training: Week 14			
Day	Workout (priority)	Duration	Pace	% $\dot{V}O_2$max	
Su	Long (1)	Max + 40 min	Moderate	60-70	
M	Recovery (4)	1/2 max + 8 min	Easy	50-60	
Tu	Recovery (6)	1/2 max + 8 min	Easy	50-60	
W	Race prep (3)	7 × 1 mile	Goal pace	90	
Th	Recovery (5)	1/2 max + 8 min	Easy	50-60	
F	Steady state or fartlek (2)	2/3 max + 10 min	SWS	75-85	
Sa	Interval or new interval (7)	5 × 200 m	Strong	90-100	

Never wear new shoes in a race. I knew a runner who was asked, on the starting line, by a shoe company to wear a shoe they developed. He finished the marathon but didn't finish in the top three, as he should have. The shoe and his feet got very hot and large blisters developed. When the race was over a trainer had to use a razor to cut the skin on the bottom of his foot from the shoe where it had become attached.

"If You mess with Mother Nature, Father Time will get you in the end." Many talented athletes have tried to burn the candle at both ends. Training too hard and failing to allow enough recovery prevented them from living up to their potential.

Marathon Training: Week 15

Day	Workout (priority)	Duration	Pace	% $\dot{V}O_2max$
Su	Long (1)	Max + 45 min	Moderate	60-70
M	Recovery (6)	1/2 max + 8 min	Easy	50-60
Tu	Speed (4)	6 × 100 m	Strong	90-110
W	Steady state or fartlek (3)	2/3 max + 10 min	SWS	75-85
Th	Recovery (7)	1/2 max + 8 min	Easy	50-60
F	Recovery (5)	1/4 max time	Easy	50-60
Sa	Tempo or out and back (2)	1/2 max	SWS to strong	85-95

Marathon Training: Week 16				
Day	Workout (priority)	Duration	Pace	% $\dot{V}O_2max$
Su	Recovery (4)	1/2 max + 10 min	Easy	50-60
M	Steady state or fartlek (1)	2/3 max + 12 min	SWS	75-85
Tu	Recovery (5)	1/2 max + 10 min	Easy	50-60
W	Steady state or fartlek (2)	1/2 max + 12 min	SWS	75-85
Th	Recovery (6)	1/2 max + 10 min	Easy	50-60
F	Steady state or fartlek (3)	2/3 max + 12 min	SWS	75-85
Sa	Recovery (7)	1/2 max + 10 min	Easy	50-60

If you want to reach a seasonal goal, you need to stay focused and make it your top priority. An Olympian I knew was invited to a race in the Caribbean in the spring before the World Championships. While there he drove a motor scooter over some back roads, which of course, he was not familiar with. He crashed, was injured, and didn't run again for the rest of the season.

A marathoner set to run the Olympic Marathon Trials the next day was strongly urged to attend a preevent dinner. She showed up and socialized, but escaped before the dinner began so she could get one more treatment from a physical therapist who came to the trials and who had helped her the previous week. She wanted to ensure she had done all she could to prepare for the race. She honored the goal.

Marathon Training: Week 17

Day	Workout (priority)	Duration	Pace	% $\dot{V}O_2$max
Su	Long (1)	Max + 45 min	Moderate	60-70
M	Recovery (4)	1/2 max + 10 min	Easy	50-60
Tu	Recovery (6)	1/2 max + 10 min	Easy	50-60
W	Race prep (3)	8 × 1 mile	Goal pace	90
Th	Recovery (5)	1/2 max + 10 min	Easy	50-60
F	Steady state or fartlek (2)	2/3 max + 12 min	SWS	75-85
Sa	Interval or new interval (7)	6 × 200 m	Strong	90-100

	Marathon Training: Week 18			
Day	Workout (priority)	Duration	Pace	% $\dot{V}O_2$max
Su	Long (1)	Max + 50 min	Moderate	60-70
M	Recovery (6)	1/2 max + 10 min	Easy	50-60
Tu	Speed (4)	8 × 100 m	Strong	90-110
W	Steady state or fartlek (3)	2/3 max + 12 min	SWS	75-85
Th	Recovery (7)	1/2 max + 10 min	Easy	50-60
F	Recovery (5)	1/4 max time	Easy	50-60
Sa	Tempo or out and back (2)	1/2 max	SWS to strong	85-95

Remember Hans Selye and his three training phases. First is the alarm stage, the single training session where you challenge your body and then let it recover. Second is the adaptation stage made up of multiple alarm phases lasting up to 11 months. If you hit the third phase, exhaustion, you have overtrained and depleted your body's resources, and you need to rest.

"Poetry, music, forests, oceans, solitude—they were what developed enormous spiritual strength. I came to realize that spirit, as much or more than physical conditioning, had to be stored up before a race."

Herb Elliott

Marathon Training: Week 19

Day	Workout (priority)	Duration	Pace	% $\dot{V}O_2$max
Su	Recovery (4)	1/2 max + 12 min	Easy	50-60
M	Steady state or fartlek (1)	2/3 max + 14 min	SWS	75-85
Tu	Recovery (5)	1/2 max + 12 min	Easy	50-60
W	Steady state or fartlek (2)	2/3 max + 14 min	SWS	75-85
Th	Recovery (6)	1/2 max + 12 min	Easy	50-60
F	Steady state or fartlek (3)	2/3 max + 14 min	SWS	75-85
Sa	Recovery (7)	1/2 max + 12 min	Easy	50-60

Marathon Training: Week 20				
Day	Workout (priority)	Duration	Pace	% $\dot{V}O_2$max
Su	Long (1)	Max + 55 min	Moderate	60-70
M	Recovery (4)	1/2 max + 12 min	Easy	50-60
Tu	Recovery (6)	1/2 max + 12 min	Easy	50-60
W	Race prep (3)	4 × 2 miles	Goal pace	90
Th	Recovery (5)	1/2 max + 12 min	Easy	50-60
F	Steady state or fartlek (2)	2/3 max + 14 min	SWS	75-85
Sa	Interval or new interval (7)	6 × 200 m	Strong	90-100

If in doubt about your pace during the first half of a goal race, be conservative. If in doubt during the second half of your race, be aggressive.

A long jumper I knew was very good and happened to jump in the era of Carl Lewis. He just couldn't beat Lewis, but then nobody could. He resolved to try to beat him, but more important, he resolved to be upbeat and do his best. He experienced a series of PBs. That's beating your best, which is what individual competition is really all about.

Marathon Training: Week 21

Day	Workout (priority)	Duration	Pace	% $\dot{V}O_2max$
Su	Long (1)	Max + 60 min	Moderate	60-70
M	Recovery (6)	1/2 max + 12 min	Easy	50-60
Tu	Speed (4)	8 × 100 m	Strong	90-110
W	Steady state or fartlek (3)	2/3 max + 14 min	SWS	75-85
Th	Recovery (7)	1/2 max + 12 min	Easy	50-60
F	Recovery (5)	1/4 max time	Easy	50-60
Sa	Tempo or out and back (2)	1/2 max	SWS to strong	85-95

	Marathon Training: Week 22			
Day	Workout (priority)	Duration	Pace	% $\dot{V}O_2$max
Su	Recovery (4)	1/2 max + 8 min	Easy	50-60
M	Steady state or fartlek (1)	2/3 max + 8 min	SWS	75-85
Tu	Recovery (5)	1/2 max + 8 min	Easy	50-60
W	Steady state or fartlek (2)	2/3 max + 8 min	SWS	75-85
Th	Recovery (6)	1/2 max + 8 min	Easy	50-60
F	Steady state or fartlek (3)	2/3 max + 8 min	SWS	75-85
Sa	Recovery (7)	1/2 max + 8 min	Easy	50-60

"What fun is it? Why all that hard, exhausting work? Where does it get you? It is one of the strange ironies of this strange life that those who work the hardest, who subject themselves to the strictest discipline, who give up certain pleasurable things in order to achieve a goal, are the happiest."

Brutus Hamilton

Under some circumstances you have to be aggressive right from the start. One year the U.S. Olympic Trials Marathon took place on a course chosen for financial reasons. It was a difficult course for athletes because the last half was mostly uphill. Experienced runners felt the only way to achieve the Olympic standard was to go out harder than usual and hang on. One runner had the courage to do that, but finished second. The course was so tough that no runner made the standard. Therefore, only the first-place runner made the Olympic team.

The runner who placed second ran the 10,000 meters at the Olympic track trials several months later. She finished fourth less than 2 seconds behind third. She had one more chance: the 5,000 meters a few days later, where she finally qualified for the Olympic team with a nice PR. Persistence paid off and justice prevailed.

Marathon Training: Week 23

Day	Workout (priority)	Duration	Pace	% $\dot{V}O_2max$
Su	Long (1)	Max + 60 min	Moderate	60-70
M	Recovery (4)	1/2 max + 8 min	Easy	50-60
Tu	Recovery (6)	1/2 max + 8 min	Easy	50-60
W	Race prep (3)	4 × 2 miles	Goal pace	90
Th	Recovery (5)	1/2 max + 8 min	Easy	50-60
F	Steady state or fartlek (2)	2/3 max + 8 min	SWS	75-85
Sa	Interval or new interval (7)	6 × 200 m	Strong	90-100

Marathon Training: Week 24

Day	Workout (priority)	Duration	Pace	% $\dot{V}O_2max$
Su	Recovery (3)	1/2 max + 4 min	Easy	50-60
M	Recovery (6)	1/2 max + 4 min	Easy	50-60
Tu	Race prep (1)	6 × 1 mile	Goal pace	90
W	Recovery (4)	1/2 max + 4 min	Easy	50-60
Th	Race prep (2)	8 × 800 m	Goal pace	90
F	Recovery (5)	1/2 max + 4 min	Easy	50-60
Sa	Recovery (7)	1/2 max + 4 min	Easy	50-60

Glucose is a key to endurance. When you run out of it, the body can't fuel the rest of the energy production process efficiently. It is a good idea to consume plenty of carbohydrate before your marathon and even to consume easily digestible food or drink as you run the marathon.

If in doubt during this week, rest instead of working too hard.

		Marathon Training: Week 25		
Day	Workout (priority)	Duration	Pace	% $\dot{V}O_2$max
Su	Long (1)	Max + 30 min	Moderate	60-70
M	Recovery (4)	1/2 max + 4 min	Easy	50-60
Tu	Interval or new interval (2)	12 × 400 m	Strong	90-100
W	Recovery (5)	1/2 max + 4 min	Easy	50-60
Th	Race prep (3)	3 × 1 mile	Goal pace	90
F	Recovery (6)	1/2 max time	Easy	50-60
Sa	Recovery (7)	1/2 max time	Easy	50-60

Marathon Training: Week 26				
Day	Workout (priority)	Duration	Pace	% $\dot{V}O_2$max
Su	Steady state or fartlek (2)	2/3 max time	Moderate	60-70
M	Recovery (4)	1/2 max time	Easy	50-60
Tu	Recovery (7)	1/2 max time	Easy	50-60
W	Speed (3)	6 × 100 m	Strong	90-110
Th	Recovery (5)	1/4 max time	Easy	50-60
F	Recovery (6)	1/4 max time	Easy	50-60
Sa	Race (1)	Marathon	Goal pace	90

If you've experienced a successful goal race, celebrate and enjoy that fact. Don't make the mistake of immediately refocusing on the next race. The longer the successful race, the longer you should relax and enjoy it!

17

Postrace Recovery and Injury Training

Progress in a running program doesn't proceed along a steady upward slope. As you climb toward peaks, you're almost certain to dip into valleys along the way.

The low spots are unplanned setbacks—usually caused by injuries or illness, but also a result of personal or work conflicts that disrupt training plans. You also encounter voluntary valleys in the form of necessary downtime after big races or hard seasons of racing. This chapter shows you how to climb out of the valleys.

Recovering From Races

Racing is hard work. It's challenging, motivating, and exciting. But as you push yourself harder in the race-day crowd than you could alone, the race takes a toll that you must repay. The longer the race, the greater the toll and the time needed to repay it. For instance, you might feel fine to run a few days after a 5K, but you might be too sore a few days after a marathon.

Just as I can't outline specific programs for returning to training after injuries, I also can't lay out exact programs for postrace recovery because it varies so widely depending on race distances. I can tell you that runners recover at fairly predictable rates as they pass through three stages of recovery. One commonly used approach is the Foster formula (named for the legendary New Zealand marathoner Jack Foster). It calls for one day of easy running for each mile of the race. For example, if your race was a 10K (6.2 miles), you need about a week to recover. If you ran a marathon (26.2 miles, or 42.2K), you'll need nearly a month for your body to heal. This doesn't mean you don't run during this recovery period, but you should avoid long or fast training and racing. Aquajogging—running in the water with a flotation device—would be a good substitute for running during this period.

For people new to running or for older runners, one easy day per *kilometer* might serve as an even better guideline. Using this formula, the recovery period works out to 10 days after a 10K and about seven weeks after a marathon.

Whether it's one day per mile or a day per kilometer, the recovery timetable accounts for the normal stages of rebuilding after an all-out effort. Each stage demands more recovery time than the one before.

1. **Stage 1: Soreness.** Certain muscles hurt the next day, and they often hurt more the day after that because of the phenomenon known as delayed-onset muscle soreness, or DOMS. Wait out this condition, which usually passes soon after it has peaked 48 to 72 hours after the race. Run little, if at all, because overworking stressed legs only invites injury. If you want to stay active, choose an activity other than running. Swimming or water running are good choices, and they help speed recovery from DOMS.

2. **Stage 2: Tiredness.** Nothing specifically hurts anymore, but you feel vaguely sluggish and low on energy. You might, after a long race, want to eat, drink, and sleep more than normal. These are signs that the body is still healing. Indulge yourself by taking nothing but easy runs, perhaps supplementing them with cross-training.

3. **Stage 3: Laziness.** Your body feels fine, but still your head isn't in the game. Your training runs aren't exciting, and you're unmotivated to try another race. Marathoners call this condition the *postmarathon blues*. This is normal and even necessary—it's the mind's way of protecting the body, forcing you to take the full quota of recovery time. You'll be ready to run another race when you forget how hard the last one felt, and then you'll regain your excitement for long and fast training.

During recovery, use the Foster formula: one day of easy running for each mile of the race.

Recovering From Injuries

Most running injuries are caused by biomechanical quirks or training mistakes. Very few are caused by accidents such as stepping into a hole or running into a dog. Instead they are brought on by the act of running. You run farther, faster, or more often than your body can handle. Or you run without giving your body a proper diet or adequate rest. It rebels by breaking down. That's the bad news.

The good news is that few injuries are serious if you catch them early, and you can usually recover from them rather quickly just by modifying your activity. I can't prescribe an exact rehab program because the degree of damage and speed of recovery vary widely from runner to runner. And the reason the interruption occurred also varies. What I can do is lay out guidelines for progressing by stages back to normal running training.

Listen closely to your body's signals, and accept pain as a friend who is telling you honestly and for your own good what you should and shouldn't do. If you try to rush progress you might end up slipping back through the stages. The list of stages of injury that follows is borrowed from Joe Henderson's book, *Running 101* (Human Kinetics, 2000). If you're coming back from an illness, substitute the word *fatigue* for *pain*, and work up from stage 2.

1. **Stage 1.** Walking is painful, but running is impossible. Bike, swim, or aqua jog during your usual running time. These activities don't put pressure on most injuries, but they still provide steady training. They let you retain some control over your physical life.

2. **Stage 2.** Walking is relatively pain free, but running still hurts. Start to walk—for the same amount of time as your normal runs—as soon as you can move ahead without limping. Continue as long as the pain is minimal. (These limitations apply at all stages of recovery.)

3. **Stage 3.** Walking is easy and some running is possible. As walking becomes too easy, add intervals of slow running—as little as 1 minute in 5 at first. Gradually build up the amount of running until you reach the next stage.

4. **Stage 4.** Running pain ceases, but minor discomfort persists. The balance tips in favor of running mixed with walking. Insert brief periods of walking at this stage when pain returns during the steady pounding from running.

5. **Stage 5.** All pain and tenderness is gone. Run again, but approach each outing cautiously for a while as you regain lost fitness. Run a little slower than normal, with no long runs or fast efforts—and very few hills and definitely no races—until you can handle the short, slow runs comfortably.

Only after you've passed stage 5 are you ready to resume normal training and racing. If you understand what caused the problem, you've learned a valuable lesson and can run smarter in the future.

Recovering From Illness

Illness is another factor that requires recovery. It is usually associated with a fever. Some people say you should train through a low-grade fever. I don't agree. I have observed that allowing the body to fight the fever with all of its resources is the most effective way to enhance recovery. When you go for a run with a fever, you divert energy away from fighting the illness and use it instead for running. Maybe you feel better right after the run, but during the run you are allowing the bug to make gains against the body's immune system. You're actually prolonging the illness. A good rule of thumb is that when you feel good again, take one more day off.

If you have only missed a few days, you can pick up the program where you would be if you had not missed any at all. Just skip the days you missed. If the illness has been a week or two, go back in training the number of weeks you missed. If you were out two weeks, go back two weeks.

You can keep training on the revised schedule until about two weeks before your race and then pick up the schedule as it would have been if you had not been sick. In other words, do the last two weeks of the regular prerace schedule.

Your body will always talk to you, giving you different clues to how it is feeling. Listen to it and your running will be safer and more satisfying. By running consistently and intelligently you will reap the significant health and emotional benefits provided by this beautiful and natural activity.

Index

Note: The italicized *f* and *t* following page numbers refer to figures and tables, respectively.

About the Author

Richard L. Brown, PhD, is a veteran coach and exercise physiologist. He has mentored championship runners at all ages, from high school to masters, and at all levels, from novice runners to Olympic athletes and world champions.

Brown has served as a personal coach to an impressive list of world-class athletes, including Shelly Steely, Suzy Favor Hamilton, Vicki Huber, and Mary Decker Slaney. He is particularly known for guiding Slaney to her double gold medals at the 1983 Helsinki World Championships. He is one of few people to have coached athletes in both the Summer and Winter Olympic Games as well as the Paralympics. He has coached athletes in six recent Olympic Games and Olympic Trials.

Brown began his career in 1963 as a three-sport coach at Bullis Preparatory School in Maryland. He continued at the United States Naval Academy, at Mt. Blue High School in Maine, and then with the Athletics West track team as a director and exercise physiologist. In 1983, Brown was head coach of the U.S. World Championship cross country team, and he has been coaching independently ever since. He has been recognized by USA Track and Field as a master coach.

Brown earned his doctorate in exercise and movement sciences from the University of Oregon in 1992. In addition to serving as lead author of two previous editions of *Fitness Running*, he has been published in multiple peer-reviewed journals on health and fitness. He is in demand as a speaker and clinician on issues related to running and fitness.

In 2001, Brown founded the Eugene Health and Performance Foundation to promote fitness and running performance internationally. He continues to be associated with that foundation while living in Eugene, Oregon.

You'll find other outstanding running resources at

www.HumanKinetics.com/running

In the U.S. call 1-800-747-4457

Australia 08 8372 0999 • Canada 1-800-465-7301
Europe +44 (0) 113 255 5665 • New Zealand 0800 222 062

HUMAN KINETICS
The Premier Publisher for Sports & Fitness
P.O. Box 5076 • Champaign, IL 61825-5076 USA

eBook
available at
HumanKinetics.com